# PRAISE FOR
# *PLANTS YOU CAN'T KILL*

"Stacy helps take the intimidation out of gardening. She uses her years of experience as a gardener and the editor of *Birds & Blooms* to help black-thumb gardeners discover the joy and satisfaction of successfully growing plants."
—Melinda Myers, horticulture expert and author of *Small Space Gardening*

"Knowledgeable? Check! Enthusiastic? Check! Practical? Check! Stacy Tornio is a passionate garden coach, teaching both new and experienced gardeners which plants to grow to ensure garden success. With Stacy's guidance, novice gardeners can no longer plead 'black thumbs!' She'll have you creating beautiful, successful gardens in no time at all!"
—Niki Jabbour, author of *Groundbreaking Food Gardens* and *The Year-Round Vegetable Gardener*

"This great new book lays out some of the most dependable plants available for our gardens, in an clear, organized way. It takes the guess work out of gardening and will certainly help people be more successful in choosing what to grow!"
—Jessi Bloom, author of *Free-Range Chicken Gardens* and *Practical PermaCulture*

"No green thumb? No worries! Author and former editor of *Birds & Blooms* magazine Stacy Tornio guides you through the garden center like a good friend, pointing out the best of the bunch. With more than 100 easy, rewarding flowers, herbs, trees, shrubs, veggies, and even houseplants to choose from, you'll soon be on your way to filling your yard with beauty, your home with greenery, and your table with homegrown goodness. Stacy's lively, down-to-earth writing will keep you going back for more as you grow into a confident gardener with *Plants You Can't Kill*."
—Sally Roth, author of *The Backyard Bird Feeder's Bible*

"Stacy's many years of gardening experience translates into a book that makes it super easy to learn about great hard-to-kill plants. Each plant entry has beautiful photography, easy-to-follow tips and insider information that progresses from annuals through perennials all the way to herbs and vegetables. It's like having a knowledgeable garden center employee at your fingertips 24/7. This is a great gardening book for beginners or anyone afraid of failure. Remember, it's okay to fail, just try again!"
—Diane Blazek, executive director, All-America Selections and National Garden Bureau

"In her many years of talking with readers of *Birds & Blooms* magazine, Stacy learned that fear of failure is one of the biggest obstacles to getting more people to garden. Her book addresses that head on by presenting beautiful, reliable plants in a simple-yet-effective way that anyone can understand, regardless of their experience level. It would make a great gift for any beginner gardener in your life."
—Susan Martin, perennial plant expert

# PLANTS YOU CAN'T KILL

## 101 EASY-TO-GROW SPECIES FOR BEGINNING GARDENERS

### STACY TORNIO

Skyhorse Publishing

Photos on pages 2, 3, 11, 20, 23, 25, 28, 34, 36, 38, 39, 40, 45, 46, 48, 50, 56, 59, 60, 62, 63, 78, 80, 82, 84, 96, 100, 101, 102, 105, 106, 115, 116, 118, 120, 122, 123, 124, 144, 148, 151, 155 used with permission from Donna Krischan.

Skyhorse Publishing books may be purchased in bulk at special discounts for sales promotion, corporate gifts, fund-raising, or educational purposes. Special editions can also be created to specifications. For details, contact the Special Sales Department, Skyhorse Publishing, 307 West 36th Street, 11th Floor, New York, NY 10018 or info@skyhorsepublishing.com.

Skyhorse® and Skyhorse Publishing® are registered trademarks of Skyhorse Publishing, Inc.®, a Delaware corporation.

Visit our website at www.skyhorsepublishing.com.

10 9 8 7 6

Library of Congress Cataloging-in-Publication Data

Names: Tornio, Stacy, author.
Title: Plants you can't kill : 101 easy-to-grow species for beginning gardeners / Stacy Tornio.
Description: New York, NY : Skyhorse Publishing, [2017] | Includes index.
Identifiers: LCCN 2016050122 (print) | LCCN 2016052563 (ebook) | ISBN 9781510709638 (alk. paper) | ISBN 9781510709690
Subjects: LCSH: Gardening.
Classification: LCC SB450.97 .T67 2017 (print) | LCC SB450.97 (ebook) | DDC 635--dc23
LC record available at https://lccn.loc.gov/2016050122

Cover design by Jennifer Ruetz, Jennifer Ruetz Graphic Design
Interior design by Jennifer Ruetz, Jennifer Ruetz Graphic Design

Printed in China

*This book is dedicated to the talented Bingham women—*
*Linda, Cherry, Wanda, Peggy, Iva, and Amanda—for their love of*
*plants and gardening.*

# DISCLAIMER

This book is not meant to challenge you to be a plant killer in any way. Yes, as the author of this book, I am quite aware that a title like *Plants You Can't Kill* is begging for you to say, "I bet I can kill it." (Believe me, I've had many, many friends tell me this already.) Even though I am quite confident in my plant selections as being hardy, resilient, tough, and hard to kill, this is where I tell you I am not responsible for your garden or plants. So if you do in fact kill some of the plants I suggest in the book, you have my deepest condolences, but I will not replace your plant or refund the money you spent on this book. Those are the breaks people. But seriously, I hope this book does help you be less of a plant killer and more of a plant thriller. Ooooo—now we're talking!

# SPECIAL THANKS

This book wouldn't have been possible without the wonderful "plant committee" I put together. Instead of just picking all the plants myself, I went to bona fide experts, which included legit horticulturalists, master gardeners, backyard gardeners, garden center workers, authors, and my mom. They gave me their top picks for easy-to-grow plant species, which got me to the final 101 list. In no particular order, I'd like to thank the following gardening experts and plant enthusiasts:

- Melinda Myers
- Vicki Schilleman
- Jessi Bloom
- Linda Lancaster
- Susan Martin
- Sally Roth
- David Mizejewski
- Amanda Shirey
- Diane Blazek
- Stephen Scott
- Niki Jabbour

I would also like to give an extra special thanks to Susan Martin. Susan is a plant expert based in Holland, Michigan. She is a lifelong gardener and has worked in the green industry for years. She reviewed the material in this book and offered valuable feedback to make it even better for the home gardener.

Finally, I want to give another special thanks to Donna Krischan. She is a garden photographer who supplied nearly half the images for this book. Not only is she talented, but she's also an excellent gardener and person. Thank you, Donna, for your kindness and photos!

# CONTENTS

# START HERE!

Gardening is not hard! It's not—seriously. I've been gardening since I was old enough to eat dirt, and if you follow a few basic rules—add sunshine, water, and don't let weeds take over—then you're pretty much guaranteed to have success.

I've heard so many excuses: "I kill everything . . ." "I don't really know what I'm doing . . ." "I don't know what to grow . . ." "I don't have a green thumb." But I promise, if you have the will, then you can definitely find a way.

My gardening experience goes way, way back. I remember both of my grandmas growing the most beautiful flowers. And my family pretty much grew and harvested every vegetable imaginable. I even had my own farmers' market stand as a kid.

Over the past decade, I've developed a new love of gardening. As the former editor of *Birds & Blooms* magazine (a fantastic magazine with more than one million subscribers), I spent ten years helping readers find plants that are good for birds, butterflies, bees, and more. I also became a master gardener during this time and got really involved in educating kids about the joys and benefits of gardening.

I've seen a *lot* of gardening books in my day, but not many are targeted to beginners. I don't know how many times I've had family or friends come to me, asking for easy, foolproof plants— ones that are nearly impossible to kill. Yet, they don't want a big, involved book to get answers. So I finally decided to write a book especially for beginners! This book is meant to start with the basics, and it focuses on some of the easiest plants known to gardeners. They look great, are reliable, and will almost guarantee you success!

I chose the plants on this list with a lot of careful thought and consideration. I used a panel of plant and gardening experts to help, and I'm extremely proud of the results. As you embark

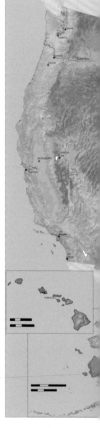

on your own gardening journey, use the chapters as a guide to help you pick the best plants for your space. Also, don't forget to consult your own local garden experts—they will know your area best and help guide you in the right direction. In addition, find your location on the USDA's Plant Hardiness Zones map, provided below and available to you on USDA.gov. (If you live in Canada, please turn to page 174 to see your map!)

Above all, plant what you like and what you love. Whether that's colorful flowers or food you can eat, the best plants you can grow are ones you like! Good luck gardening . . . and not killing the plants!

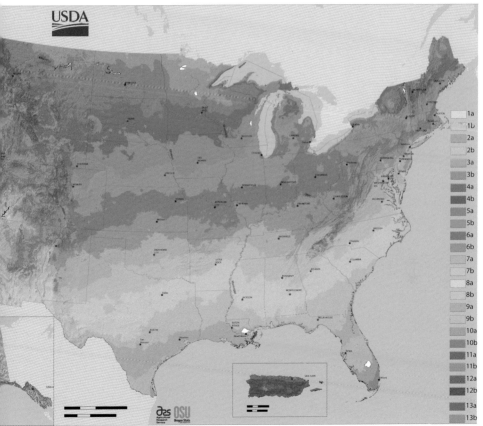

**What's a Zone Map?**

Most plants you buy (not annuals, though) will list recommended zones.
If you're unsure of your zone, check it on this map.

# ANNUALS

Hello to the annuals! You might be thinking, "Wait, don't annuals naturally die every year? Why are they in a book about plants you can't kill?" Okay, wise guy or gal, this might be true, but they're still worth having in the backyard. Annuals are particularly popular because they offer great color in a short amount of time. Plus, they are fantastic in containers and pots! Here are some of the toughest annuals you can grow in your backyard.

# ZINNIA

## PROFILE

Zinnias are one of the most cost-effective flowers you can grow in your backyard. A single pack of seeds can yield dozens of colorful blooms from summer through fall. Although they are known to attract butterflies, bees, and even hummingbirds, you'll probably want to plant some extra for yourself because they make excellent cut flowers. Many gardeners also love growing these in containers. This is a plant that loves sunshine, so keep it watered, and it'll thrive in even the hottest conditions.

## STATS

| Common Name | Zinnia |
| --- | --- |
| Botanical Name | *Zinnia elegans* |
| Height | 1 to 4 feet |
| Spread | up to 1 foot |
| Flower Color | Orange, pink, purple, red, white, yellow, green, and multicolor |
| Light Needs | Full sun |

### GREEN THUMB TIP

Zinnias do tend to be affected by a plant disease called powdery mildew, so when you buy seeds (or plants), look for varieties listed as disease-resistant.

### ✓ TOP PICKS

Green flowers?!? Yes, they exist in the world of zinnias! Look for these two cultivars—Envy and Tequila Lime—if you want something a bit out of the ordinary.

# CELOSIA

## PROFILE

If you garden in USDA zones 10 or 11, you can grow celosia year-round, but for the rest of us, we plant it as an annual. The beautiful, bushy flowers are unlike anything else in the garden, and they love the summer heat. So while lots of other plants will start to fade, celosia will still be going strong. This plant's flowers are a bit feathery, which is also attractive to butterflies and bees.

## STATS

| | |
|---|---|
| Common Name | Celosia, Cockscomb |
| Botanical Name | *Celosia argentea* |
| Height | 6 inches to more than 2 feet |
| Spread | up to 18 inches |
| Flower Color | Silvery white, red, orange, yellow, pink, purple |
| Light Needs | Full sun |

## 🍃 GREEN THUMB TIP

If you want to really make an impact in the garden, plant several different colors of celosia in one spot. The varying shades of red, orange, yellow, pink, and purple really stand out!

## ➥ GARDEN HISTORY

The common name for celosia—cockscomb—earned this name because it resembles a rooster's comb.

# GERANIUM

## PROFILE

It wouldn't be summer without geraniums. They are one of those blooms that look great from spring through late fall. A few people (USDA zones 10 and 11) are lucky enough to grow this as a perennial, but for the rest of us, we usually buy them new each year. While they'll tolerate both sun and partly cloudy, be sure to keep them watered and plant them in well-drained soil. (So if you are planting them in containers, make sure there is drainage in the bottom of the pot.) By planting geraniums, you can also say you're helping support the bee population because they'll appreciate them all season.

## STATS

| Common Name | Geranium |
|---|---|
| Botanical Name | *Pelargonium* |
| Height | up to 3 feet |
| Spread | up to 3 feet |
| Flower Color | Red, orange, pink, purple, white, bicolor |
| Light Needs | Part shade to full sun |

### GREEN THUMB TIP

You can make a spectacular red, white, and blue display with geraniums. Just get white and red blooms and plant them in a bright blue pot. It's a great way to show off your patriotic side.

### GARDEN CHALLENGE

Some gardeners have had success saving their geraniums through winter. They do this in one of two ways: they'll take cuttings in fall and root them inside, or they will cut the plant back and grow it as a houseplant in spring. It's a little tricky, but it's worth a try!

---

DEADHEADING IS A FANCY TERM IN THE GARDENING WORLD, WHICH JUST MEANS PINCHING OFF OLD FLOWERS SO NEW ONES CAN GROW. DO THIS WITH YOUR GERANIUMS TO KEEP BLOOMS NEW, FRESH, AND GORGEOUS.

Coleus is easy to start from a cutting. Just dip the cutting in some rooting hormone, then plant and water.

# COLEUS

Flowers tend to get all the attention, but coleus proves that foliage can be sexy, too. This plant actually has tropical origins, and it's easy to see with its bright and showy colors. It has been cultivated time and time again to produce the coolest foliage. You can seriously find hundreds of different coleus on the market today. As a bonus, it thrives in both sun and shade, so these plants are fantastic in containers on decks or patios that get either little or lots of sunshine.

## STATS

| Common Name | Coleus |
|---|---|
| Botanical Name | *Solenostemon* |
| Height | up to 3 feet |
| Spread | 2 to 4 feet |
| Flower Color | Not grown for flowers, but if they do bloom, small purplish or white blooms |
| Foliage Color | Nearly every color imaginable except blue |
| Light Needs | Sun or shade |

### 🌀 GREEN THUMB TIP

Mix your coleus! By combining two very different foliage colors like a deep red with a bright green, you'll get a gorgeous end result.

### ✓ TOP PICKS

To each their own when it comes to coleus. With so many cultivars to choose from, you really owe it to yourself to do some Googling to find what best suits you. Watermelon is a type with beautiful pinkish foliage. Or look for Chocolate Mint with rich green and brown leaves.

### ➤➤ GARDEN HISTORY

Botanists believe coleus originated in Southeast Asia. The German-Dutch botanist, Karl Ludwig von Blume is known for introducing it to Europe in the nineteenth century.

# WAX BEGONIA

## PROFILE

You can find many begonias on the market today, but wax begonias are definitely most popular among home gardeners. They are low-maintenance and have a bit of a tropical look to them. They are especially known for surviving and thriving in dry, hot conditions. With begonias, go by the rule that more is better. Don't just plant one—try planting five or six instead!

## STATS

| Common Name | Wax begonias, bedding begonias |
|---|---|
| Botanical Name | *Begonia × semperflorens-cultorum* |
| Height | up to 1 foot |
| Spread | up to 1 foot |
| Flower Color | White, pink, red, bicolor |
| Foliage Color | Thick, shiny leaves that can look like wax; foliage can be a rich green or even a purplish color |
| Light Needs | Sun or shade |

## GREEN THUMB TIP

If you live in an area where summers get really hot for prolonged periods, then your begonias should be planted in an area that gets some shade. This will help them survive and thrive.

# MOSS ROSE

## PROFILE

Think of this plant as a cross between roses and cactus. The blooms look a bit like roses and a bit like the flowers you'd find on a cactus. It has spiky, succulent-type leaves, and it does really well in sunny, dry, hot conditions—much like a desert. The hotter and drier it is, the better this plant will do. Keep this in mind and you'll definitely have success. Even though it's an annual, it will often reseed, so don't be surprised if you see moss roses popping up from one year to the next.

## STATS

| Common Name | Moss rose |
|---|---|
| Botanical Name | *Portulaca grandiflora* |
| Height | 4 to 8 inches |
| Spread | 6 inches to 2 feet |
| Flower Color | Red, orange, yellow, pink, purple, white |
| Light Needs | Full sun |

## GREEN THUMB TIP

If you have a rocky area where you can't seem to get anything to grow, then moss rose is the plant for you. It doesn't need perfect soil and actually thrives in these conditions.

ON A CLOUDY DAY, THE BLOOMS WILL CLOSE. BUT WHEN IT'S SUNNY AGAIN, THEY OPEN BACK UP.

# PETUNIA

## PROFILE

You won't find a plant that produces more blooms in a single season. The flowers start in spring, and then they last well into summer and fall. Known to attract butterflies, bees, and hummingbirds, this is without a doubt one of the most popular annuals. It works great in containers, in the front of garden beds, and sprinkled throughout other areas to provide pops of color wherever needed. One of the best things about petunias is they'll grow in a variety of soil conditions, further solidifying their popularity among gardeners.

## STATS

| Common Name | Petunia |
|---|---|
| Botanical Name | *Petunia* |
| Height | up to 2 feet |
| Spread | up to 3 feet |
| Flower Color | Pretty much every color imaginable except brown, as well as bicolor varieties |
| Light Needs | Full sun to part shade |

## 🌑 GREEN THUMB TIP

If you want your petunias to look good all season, try feeding them regularly with a water-soluble plant food. You can get this at your local garden center, and it'll really give them the boost they need to look great for months.

## ✓ TOP PICKS

The best and coolest petunias can't really be started from seed because they are considered hybrids. (Modern hybrids don't really require deadheading to bloom all season, too!) One of the best lines of new varieties is the Supertunia. Look at www.provenwinners.com to see some of those options.

According to Guinness World Records, the tallest sunflower to date is 30 feet and 1 inch.

# SUNFLOWER

Want a plant to grow directly and successfully from seed? This is it! Just take a walk down your seed aisle, and you'll see a few dozen options for sunflowers—then just sow directly into the ground and wait for the magic to happen. And these aren't necessarily the sunflowers that you remember from your childhood. Sure, you can find those classic tall blooms with giant seed heads, but there are many more options on the market today, including dwarf plants that are only a foot or two tall. By the way, birds love 'em and so do bees and butterflies, yet more reasons to grow this classic garden favorite.

## STATS

| Common Name | Sunflower |
|---|---|
| Botanical Name | *Helianthus annuus* |
| Height | Can vary from a few feet to more than 10 feet tall |
| Spread | 1 to 3 feet |
| Flower Color | Varying shades of yellow, red, and plenty of cool bicolor options |
| Light Needs | Full sun |

### GREEN THUMB TIP

Before these blooms completely die off in fall, consider cutting off the flower heads, and put them in a garage, shed, or basement to dry. Save a few of those seeds to plant next year, and then put out the dried seed heads in winter, which will make the birds really happy!

### ✓ TOP PICKS

For a deep red option, look for Moulin Rouge. Mammoth Russian is one of the tallest varieties on the market today. Finally, look for Lemon Queen, a sunflower variety known for supporting pollinators.

### ➤ GARDEN HISTORY

Sunflowers peeked in popularity in the nineteenth century in Russia. By the late part of the century, they started making their way to the United States—the Mammoth Russian sunflower was a popular option in seed catalogs dating back to 1880. In addition, this flower has a long history of being good for healing.

# CALIFORNIA POPPY

## PROFILE

As the state flower of California, this poppy grows as a perennial for many (hardy to zone 6), but many gardeners still grow it as an annual. When you plant several of these in one spot, it has a huge impact, making for a gorgeous sea of orange blooms. Gardeners will often do this in dry spots that don't get a lot of water because this is one of the most drought-tolerant plants you can find. They also do well in sandy conditions, which can be a challenge for some (you know who you are). California poppies are native to the United States, so it's pretty common to see them growing wild, especially in the West.

## STATS

| Common Name | California poppy |
|---|---|
| Botanical Name | *Eschscholzia californica* |
| Height | 1 to 2 feet |
| Spread | 1 to 2 feet |
| Flower Color | Orange to orange-yellow |
| Light Needs | Full sun |

## 🌱 GREEN THUMB TIP

You can sow seeds directly into the ground in spring or you can plant them in the fall just before frost.

# SWEET POTATO VINE

## PROFILE

Here's another plant you grow for the foliage and not the flowers. In fact, it's one of *the* most popular plants for containers. When you have a container, it's nice to have colorful flowers that grow up (often called *thrillers*) mixed with interesting and contrasting foliage plants (often called *spillers*). Sweet potato vine does exactly that, spilling over hanging baskets or pots to add visual interest and great color. Some gardeners will even use it as a groundcover, letting it trail in and out of their garden beds.

## STATS

| Common Name | Sweet potato vine |
| --- | --- |
| Botanical Name | *Ipomoea batatas* |
| Height | Up to 1 foot |
| Spread | Up to 10 feet |
| Flower Color | Rarely flowers |
| Foliage Color | Beautiful, rich foliage that can come in shades of green, purple, and more |
| Light Needs | Full sun to part shade |

## GARDEN HISTORY

Sweet potato vines have these orange tubers that people have been harvesting and eating for more than two thousand years. You may find small tubers in your container when you empty it out in the fall, but most ornamental sweet potato vines do not form actual potatoes.

# COSMOS

## PROFILE

You can't get any more low maintenance than the cosmos. You can seriously just throw some seeds out into the garden, and they'll likely come up with little care or attention from you. The daisy-like blooms can get a bit top heavy, but if you grow them in a bunch, they'll naturally support one another. Oh yeah—butterflies adore cosmos, so don't be surprised if you see big swallowtails stopping by for nectar.

## STATS

| Common Name | Cosmos, Mexican aster |
|---|---|
| Botanical Name | *Cosmos bipinnatus* |
| Height | up to 4 feet |
| Spread | up to 3 feet |
| Flower Color | Red, pink, white, yellow |
| Light Needs | Full sun |

### 🌼 GREEN THUMB TIP

Technically, this plant is an annual, but it often reseeds on its own every year, so consider that a bonus! This gives you an excuse to leave it up in your garden through fall and winter instead of cleaning it out. This way, it'll continue to attract wildlife, and those seeds can fall to the ground and get ready to give you more cosmos next year!

### ✓ TOP PICKS

Xanthos is a relatively new variety with its buttery shade, making it the first time it's been available in a shade of yellow. Rubinato is also relatively new and deep red. The Seashells Mix has fascinating petals that resemble tubular seashells.

# SWEET ALYSSUM

## PROFILE

Don't be fooled by the tiny little flowers on this relatively small plant. They bloom in bunches and pack a strong punch of fragrance (hence the "sweet" as part of the name). Because they don't take up much space, they make a great filler plant in containers, flower beds, and anywhere else you need to tuck in some color. They peak early for color in spring and may fade back a bit in summer, but be patient because they'll often perk back up in fall. You can also just sow some more seeds in late summer for an extra bloom show in autumn.

## STATS

| Common Name | Sweet alyssum, alyssum, carpet flower |
| --- | --- |
| Botanical Name | *Lobularia maritima* |
| Height | just a few inches up to 1 foot |
| Spread | up to 1 foot |
| Flower Color | White |
| Light Needs | Full sun to part shade |

## ✓ TOP PICKS

Sweet alyssum is best known for its white blooms, but new varieties are hitting the plant world every year, now offering shades of pink, magenta, and purple.

# SAGE

Some might put sage in the herbs section while others will say it belongs with perennials. Technically, it could fall in both since some gardeners get it to come back every year and others grow it for the herbal or cooking benefits. However, this member of the mint family is also a popular annual, perfect in many scenarios. Attractive to both bees and butterflies, you can use it to fill holes in perennial beds, garden borders, and containers.

## STATS

| | |
|---|---|
| Common Name | Culinary sage, common sage, garden sage |
| Botanical Name | *Salvia officinalis* |
| Height | up to 2 or 3 feet |
| Spread | up to 2 or 3 feet |
| Flower Color | Blue, purple |
| Light Needs | Full sun |

## GREEN THUMB TIP

There's one main thing you need to remember when it comes to sage—don't let the soil get too wet.

## ✓ TOP PICKS

Related to common sage is pineapple sage (*Salvia elegans*). As you might guess, its foliage has a pineapple scent when crushed—seriously. It can grow up to 5 feet and is very popular with butterflies and hummingbirds.

Many gardeners consider snapdragons to be deer-resistant.

# SNAPDRAGON

## PROFILE

The snapdragon is considered a tender perennial, which means it could come back if you live in zones 7 and up. However, it's definitely sensitive to the cold, so you should probably just think of it as an annual. No worries—this is one of the most common annuals on the market today, and your garden center should have lots of six-packs for relatively cheap. Plant these early (March or April in some areas) for blooms that will last into October or even November. They might take a break from blooming in summer, but then they'll resurge in the fall. Now that's some good bang for your buck!

## STATS

| Common Name | Snapdragon |
|---|---|
| Botanical Name | *Antirrhinum majus* |
| Height | up to 3 feet |
| Spread | up to 1 foot |
| Flower Color | White, yellow, orange, purple, pink, red, purple, bicolor |
| Light Needs | Full sun |

## ● GREEN THUMB TIP

Snapdragons will keep blooming and blooming with a little help from you. Just keep deadheading those fading flowers, and new ones will keep appearing for months.

## ✓ TOP PICKS

One of the newest snapdragons on the market is in a line called Candy Showers. It's the first snapdragon to be grown from seed as a trailing plant, which makes it perfect for a hanging basket. You can find it in several different colors, including deep purple, orange, white, yellow, red, and rose.

## ➤→GARDEN HISTORY

How did this plant get its name? Take a close look and you'll see that the flower itself looks like it has a bit of a snout, much like a dragon. In fact, if you take your fingers and squeeze, it even looks like the dragon is snapping its mouth open and shut!

Pinch back old flowers to encourage new ones throughout the growing season.

# FLOWERING TOBACCO

## PROFILE

Love hummingbirds? The flowering tobacco is like a secret weapon when it comes to attracting them. Often overlooked, this annual with star-shaped, tubular blooms is like a magnet to them. If you like fragrant flowers, then you'll reap some of the rewards, too. These are some of the best scented flowers you can buy, so take a deep breath when you're outside, and you're sure to get a whiff of pure sweetness. On sunny days, the blooms actually close up. This might seem counterintuitive, but it's guaranteed to make your garden more interesting!

## STATS

| Common Name | Flowering tobacco, tobacco, ornamental tobacco |
|---|---|
| Botanical Name | *Nicotiana alata* |
| Height | up to 5 feet |
| Spread | up to 2 feet |
| Flower Color | White, red, yellow, green, pink |
| Light Needs | Full sun to part shade |

## 🌑 GREEN THUMB TIP

If your flowering tobacco really shoots up and is having a great year of flower production, then consider staking the plants to keep them healthy and strong. Also, keep this one away from pets or small kids because the plants do have poisonous parts.

## ✓ TOP PICKS

A few years ago, the Perfume Series came out (look for botanical name, *Nicotiana × sanderae*). Perfume Deep Purple won an All-America Selections award because it has great fragrance, and you don't need to pinch blooms to keep them looking great.

## ➤→GARDEN HISTORY

So what's with tobacco in the name? Yes, it is related to the tobacco plant grown for smoking tobacco. They are in the same plant family, Nicotiana, and all of these plants do contain a high concentration of nicotine.

# PANSY

## PROFILE

There are so, so many reasons to love pansies. First of all, they're one of the earliest flowers to grace garden centers in spring. This means if you're plant-hungry and sick of winter, you can sneak some pansies on your patio, and even if you have some cold nights ahead, they're probably going to make it just fine. Second, they have a "dog-like face" that many gardeners adore. Now add on that they're relatively maintenance-free, and you'll be jumping on the pansy bandwagon, too.

## STATS

| Common Name | Pansy |
|---|---|
| Botanical Name | *Viola × wittrockiana* |
| Height | up to 10 inches |
| Spread | up to 1 foot |
| Flower Color | Red, orange, yellow, blue, violet, white, pink, bicolors, and even tricolors |
| Light Needs | Full sun to part shade |

## GREEN THUMB TIP

They actually thrive in cooler temps, so if it gets really hot, give them a break inside a porch or patio. Some people will use pansies as a late summer/early fall flower, too, treating it almost like you would a chrysanthemum. They can really add to an autumn display because the blooms can take those cooler nights.

## ✓ TOP PICKS

One of the few plants that offer a black bloom, look for the Black Moon cultivar.

# SPIDER FLOWER

## PROFILE

For better or for worse, once you have spider flower in your garden, you might always have it. The plant gets its name because the blooms look a bit like spiders with spidery "legs" coming off the main flower. Definitely take a chance at growing these from seed. You can pretty much sprinkle them wherever you want, and they'll likely come up and produce gorgeous flowers for the bees and butterflies. You can also find plants, especially of some of the new varieties, at your local garden center.

## STATS

| Common Name | Spider flower, cleome |
|---|---|
| Botanical Name | *Cleome hassleriana* |
| Height | up to 6 feet |
| Spread | up to 2 feet |
| Flower Color | Pink, purple, white, bicolors |
| Light Needs | Full sun to part shade |

## ✓ TOP PICKS

Look for hybrid cleomes in these two series: Queen and Sparkler. Sparklers are known for being more compact, and they'll even do well in containers. Queen are grown for their rich and colorful blooms.

---

KIDS LOVE THIS PLANT BECAUSE OF THE FLOWER'S SPIDERY LEGS. IT'S A GREAT START TO CREATING AN "ANIMAL GARDEN," WHICH INCLUDES PLANTS WITH ANIMALS IN THE NAMES.

---

# MARIGOLD

## PROFILE

The marigold might take the top honor for being one of the most drought-resistant, heat-tolerant blooms in the garden. It doesn't seem to matter how hot it gets because the marigold survives and thrives. If you go to the garden center in spring, you'll likely find them selling marigolds by the flat, which might include up to twenty-four plants. Go ahead and buy the whole thing! This is one of those plants that do great just about anywhere you put it—with your annuals, in containers, or to have as a filler in your perennial beds— so you know it's not going to go to waste. For an even a better display and strong impact, plant several different colors of marigolds in one area.

## STATS

| Common Name | Marigold, French marigold |
|---|---|
| Botanical Name | *Tagetes patula* |
| Height | up to 1 foot |
| Spread | 6 to 8 inches |
| Flower Color | Yellow, orange, red, bicolor |
| Light Needs | Full sun |

## GREEN THUMB TIP

How do you choose one marigold over another? These French marigolds are probably the most common, but another species called pot marigolds (look for the botanical name *Calendula*) is also pretty common. They have a similar look, though they usually get taller. Gardeners grow them for their edible flowers. (There's also a third kind called the African marigold.) If you're at the garden store and are unsure what you're buying, just look at the label for the botanical name or ask one of the workers.

## ✓ TOP PICKS

Attract beneficial insects to your garden by planting a couple different cultivars of French marigolds. Look for Red Metamorph and Disco.

# LANTANA

## PROFILE

Here's another annual that is tropical in appearance—for good reason, too. Lantana in native to the Caribbean, and you might even find it growing year-round in warm areas of California or Florida. This is a bloom that is like fine wine, getting better with time. The small clusters of flowers usually start out as a soft, single color. Then as the plant ages, they change color and deepen. Grow it in a sunny spot, and you'll love watching it thrive as some of your other blooms fade in the heat of the summer. Don't let the tiny little flowers fool you; they pack a big punch. Butterflies love them—they have a thing for tubular blooms like you get on lantana.

## STATS

| Common Name | Lantana, yellow sage |
|---|---|
| Botanical Name | *Lantana camara* |
| Height | up to 4 feet |
| Spread | up to 3 feet |
| Flower Color | Red, orange, yellow, purple, white, pink, bicolor |
| Foliage Color | Nearly every color imaginable except blue |
| Light Needs | Full sun |

### ● GREEN THUMB TIP

Lantana is considered a bit aggressive in certain areas. If you're worried about this, plant it in a space that can be contained or leave it in a pot. It also does great in a hanging basket.

### ✓ TOP PICKS

Want variety in your flower color? Look for Feston Rose, a pink and yellow option, or Radiation for red and orange blooms.

# MEXICAN SUNFLOWER

## PROFILE

Though they aren't actually in the sunflower family, this native to Mexico still uses the name. It's easy to write them off as just another sunflower, but don't! They definitely deserve their own spot in your flower bed, and they're just as easy to grow from seed as the sunflowers you're probably already familiar with. They produce beautiful orange blooms in even the hottest conditions while also attracting bees and butterflies. They're also a popular cut flowers if you're the type who likes to put together your own bouquets.

## STATS

| | |
|---|---|
| Common Name | Mexican sunflower |
| Botanical Name | *Tithonia rotundifolia* |
| Height | up to 6 feet |
| Spread | up to 3 feet |
| Flower Color | Orange |
| Light Needs | Full sun |

## GREEN THUMB TIP

Don't lump this in to the sunflower group. Watch the botanical names, especially if you see something that looks like it at the garden store, and make room for both. You'll be glad you did!

## ✓ TOP PICKS

Look for the Arcadian Blend, which is a more compact (just 2 or 3 feet) option in the garden.

# FAQS ON ANNUALS

## Don't annuals die every year?

Why, yes. Yes, they do. And even though this book has "plants you can't kill" in the title, you should still have annuals as part of your garden plan. However, you can save seeds from your annuals from one year to the next, so this is kind of like the plants living on. It'll definitely save you money!

## If I water my annuals more, will they grow taller?

For nearly all the plants listed, the size isn't really tied to how much you water them. Height and spread are usually specific to a certain cultivar or variety. Check plant labels when you buy to see what a typical size is for that plant.

## Why would I spend money on plants that die every year?

Because they're awesome, that's why. Annuals are known for producing gorgeous, vibrant flowers all season long. So if you like pretty things, annuals are on the list!

## What's the best use for annuals?

You can use annuals just about anywhere—in flower beds, in hanging baskets, mixed in your perennials beds—just wherever you want or need the color. They are very versatile!

## What's the best benefit about annuals?

The flowers themselves are definitely one of the top benefits. In addition, they also produce really great color in a short amount of time. A lot of times, you'll buy annuals at the garden center already in bloom and looking fantastic. So you just bring them home, and they keep right on blooming and adding color for months!

## Are annuals worth it?

Whether you grow annuals from seed or buy the plants at the store, they're definitely worth it. Just because they will likely die that year doesn't make them a bad investment. You really get so much color! They are a sure thing if you want to brighten up the front of your house or patio.

# PERENNIALS

Perennials are the true superstars of the garden. They are extremely reliable, coming back year after year, and gardeners truly rely on them to make their flower beds look great. If you ask a gardener what their favorite perennial is, they'll likely give you a list of five, six, or more—it's next to impossible to pick just one! There are just too many good options to be had—good news for you! Here are some of the easiest-to-grow, most resilient, and toughest perennials you can get for your garden.

If you cut a stem or leaf, this plant will give off a milky substance.

# MILKWEED

## PROFILE

Do not be fooled by *weed* in the name of this plant. While some gardeners might call this perennial aggressive, it's actually making a comeback as an appealing and must-have plant in the backyard. Traditionally, you've probably seen it growing in open fields or alongside the road. However, gardeners are now seeking it out because of the benefits it provides to the monarch population. Milkweed is the host plant for monarch caterpillars, so this plant is absolutely essential to ensure their long-term success. (The population has actually been dwindling, so gardeners are taking action.)

## STATS

| Common Name | Milkweed, common milkweed |
| --- | --- |
| Botanical Name | *Asclepias syriaca* |
| Zone | 3 to 9 |
| Height | 2 to 5 feet |
| Spread | up to 1 foot |
| Flower Color | Pink, white |
| Light Needs | Full sun |

## GREEN THUMB TIP

You can definitely grow milkweed from seed, but if you have a hard time getting it established, opt for plants instead. If your local garden center doesn't offer milkweed, then try ordering it online.

## ✓ TOP PICKS

Here's where a little research with your state or local native plants chapter will really come in handy. Figure out which milkweed is native to your area and plant it. Many native plants organizations will have online resources or spring plant sales, and milkweed is definitely a plant you'll want to buy directly from them.

# HENS AND CHICKS

## PROFILE

This plant is closely related to the succulent family, and gardeners love it for its unique foliage. The best thing about this plant is that it's very forgiving. You can grow it in sandy or rocky conditions, and it'll do just fine. You can also forget to water it from time to time, and it'll keep right on growing. It grows very low to the ground until the main part of the plant (the hen) sends up a stout flower stalk in summer. Little offshoots (called *chicks*) will pop up all around the "hen" as the plant matures. It's really unlike anything you've ever seen in a garden, so if you like unique, this one is definitely for you!

## STATS

| | |
|---|---|
| Common Name | Hens and chicks |
| Botanical Name | *Sempervivum* |
| Zone | 3 to 8 |
| Height | 3 to 4 inches |
| Spread | up to 2 feet |
| Flower Color | Red, purple, pink |
| Light Needs | Full sun to light shade |

## GREEN THUMB TIP

It also does well in shallow conditions. So if you want to put it in a container or in a rocky flower bed, it doesn't need a lot of soil depth to grow well. Definitely don't overwater this plant. That's one of the biggest issues gardeners have.

# RUSSIAN SAGE

## PROFILE

In 1995, this plant earned the honor of being the perennial plant of the year! Here's why—it's drought-tolerant, has hardly any disease or insect problems, and it's great for attracting butterflies and bees. Also as a bonus, Russian sage can thrive in a wide variety of soil types, so you don't have to have perfect conditions for it to look good. The tiny purplish blooms on this plant are all over from base to tip, so it really makes a statement from midsummer through fall.

## STATS

| Common Name | Russian sage |
| --- | --- |
| Botanical Name | *Perovskia atriplicifolia* |
| Zone | 4 to 9 |
| Height | 2½ to 5 feet |
| Spread | 2 to 4 feet |
| Flower Color | Purple, lavender blue |
| Light Needs | Full sun |

## GREEN THUMB TIP

When it grows big and tall, it tends to flop. For this reason, it's best to put it in the back of flower beds. It can even help support other plants, too.

# BEE BALM

## PROFILE

If you're trying to support the diminishing bee population (it's a serious problem!), bee balm is a good place to start. It definitely attracts bees and is also very popular among hummingbirds. The blooms of this plant look so cool in the way they spread out. This is one of the best native plants you can grow—there are great native options in just about every part of the country, so look for those, too. Hit up your local garden center and start bringing in the birds, butterflies, and bees into your yard!

## STATS

| Common Name | Bee balm, monarda |
| --- | --- |
| Botanical Name | *Monarda didyma* |
| Zone | 4 to 9 |
| Height | 1 to 5 feet |
| Spread | 1 to 3 feet |
| Flower Color | Red, pink, purple, lavender |
| Light Needs | Full sun to part shade |

### GREEN THUMB TIP

Like many perennials, bee balm benefit from being divided every few years. So as it multiplies, consider splitting it and sharing it with friends. Your friends get new plants, and you're encouraging the overall health of your bee balm.

### ✓ BONUS TIP

Bee balm has a reputation for getting a disease called powdery mildew. The best way to ensure your plant doesn't get this is by making sure it has good air circulation. Don't crowd it! You can also look for disease-resistant cultivars.

# TULIP

Tulips popping up all across landscapes and gardens is one true sign of spring. If you want this to be the case in your yard, you'll have to plant them in fall because they need to spend the cold winter in the ground before they can bloom in spring. Dig a hole three to four times deeper than the bulb itself and drop it in, pointy side up. You'll want to do this before the ground is frozen or too hard to dig. You can get tulips in any color you want (except blue), so happy shopping.

## STATS

| Common Name | Tulip |
|---|---|
| Botanical Name | *Tulipa* |
| Zone | 3 to 8 |
| Height | 6 inches to 2 feet |
| Spread | up to 1 foot |
| Flower Color | All colors except blue |
| Light Needs | Full sun |

## GREEN THUMB TIP

Many of the new tulip cultivars are gorgeous, but they don't last as long as the other varieties—some even just consider them annuals. Keep this in mind when planting. If you want a true perennial, talk to your garden center and ask them to recommend cultivars that will last for several years.

## ✓ TOP PICKS

Tulips are actually split into several different categories, and knowing a few of your options can really help when you're planning your garden. For instance, parrot tulips have ruffled petals. Darwins are taller, reaching more than 2 feet. Doubles are just how they sound—they have double blooms. And then the singles can either be late or early on bloom time. Read the labels when you're buying bulbs.

The botanical name *Hemerocallis* comes from two Greek words—one means "beauty" and the other means "day."

# DAYLILY

Daylilies have the great foliage of an ornamental grass while also producing beautiful and colorful blooms. While flowers only last for a day (hence the name), it seems as though they have an endless supply of blooms because they really keep going and going all summer. It doesn't need much care at all. Plus, many gardeners consider them drought-tolerant. In addition, you can get them in a huge range of colors. In fact, there's a whole society out there that celebrates this plant (check 'em out at www.daylilies.org).

## STATS

| Common Name | Daylily |
|---|---|
| Botanical Name | *Hemerocallis* |
| Zone | 3 to 9 |
| Height | 1 to 3 feet |
| Spread | 1 to 3 feet |
| Flower Color | Nearly every color except blue |
| Light Needs | Full sun to part shade |

## 🌑 GREEN THUMB TIP

Daylilies work best in groups. Plant your favorite varieties 18 to 24 inches apart. This will give them plenty of space to grow, and it'll create a nice area of your garden with great foliage.

## ✓ TOP PICKS

There are so many daylily options on the market that it's really hard to pick just a few to recommend. One of the most popular and famous daylilies is Stella de Oro, which has gorgeous golden yellow blooms and is pretty much maintenance-free. Happy Returns is lemon yellow, but it has ruffled petals. Little Business has beautiful red blooms on a smaller plant overall. Tiger Time is a stunning orange cultivar.

# HOPS

Hops—the magical plant used to make beer! If you're into home brewing at all, then you have to add hops to your list of plants to grow. It's a vining, trailing plant, and it can actually create really good privacy or interest growing along a fence. Think of it as an excellent alternative to ivy. The only tricky thing about hops is that it is *dioecious*. This means you need to plant both a male and female variety to get the hops fruit. Order online so you know you have both, or talk to someone at your local nursery.

## STATS

| Common Name | Common hop, hops |
|---|---|
| Botanical Name | *Humulus lupulus* |
| Zone | 4 to 8 feet |
| Height | 15 to 20 feet |
| Spread | 3 to 6 feet |
| Flower Color | Green |
| Light Needs | Full sun to part shade |

## 🌑 GREEN THUMB TIP

If you grow hops in order to harvest it for beer, do a little reading about what is involved. Basically, you're collecting the cone-like structures (called *strobiles*) from the female plants. This happens in the fall. If you collect them properly, then you can use them to make beer. Otherwise, just enjoy hops as a great vine for your backyard.

# VERONICA

## PROFILE

With Veronica, it seems like people fall into one of two camps—either they know about it and love it or they aren't familiar with it at all. You definitely want to be in that first camp, though. Veronica is a striking plant with tall, spiky blooms that look great throughout the summer. In addition, it's a must-have plant for any butterfly garden—not a day will go by during which you won't see a butterfly stop off for some nectar.

## STATS

| Common Name | Veronica |
|---|---|
| Botanical Name | *Veronica* |
| Zone | 4 to 9 |
| Height | 1 to 2½ feet |
| Spread | 1 to 2 feet |
| Flower Color | Purple, blue, pink, white |
| Light Needs | Full sun |

## 🌼 GREEN THUMB TIP

For people who love blue plants, you just might be able to get it with Veronica. Cultivars like Crater Lake Blue and Sunny Border Blue will get you that blue hue you're after that is so hard to achieve in the plant world.

Have a deer problem? They love hostas, so be aware of this if you're planting.

# HOSTA

## PROFILE

The hosta is the most celebrated plant among gardeners who have shade. Everyone seems to have those areas of their yard that don't see much sun, and hostas are some of the best plants that will survive and thrive in those conditions. Hallelujah! Don't write hostas off as being boring or ordinary in any way. Sure, they've been around for years, but there are so many options available today. You can get all kinds of different leaf colors, shapes, patterns, and textures. Plus, many have a pretty great offshoot of flowers, too.

## STATS

| Common Name | Hosta |
|---|---|
| Botanical Name | *Hosta* |
| Zone | 3 to 8 |
| Height | 4 inches to 4 feet |
| Spread | 6 inches to 6 feet |
| Flower Color | Grown for foliage with purple or white blooms |
| Light Needs | Sun to shade, depending on cultivar |

## GREEN THUMB TIP

Divide and conquer when it comes to hostas. They will get bigger and better every year, plus they thrive on new growth. So plan on dividing and transplanting them every three to five years into new areas. Or ask gardening friends if they have any hostas they want to share to expand your garden. If you do this, you could have a whole garden full of hostas without spending much money at all.

## ✓ TOP PICKS

With thousands of options out there, it's hard to narrow them down, but here are a couple to look for: Great Expectations is a bold hosta that changes colors from summer to autumn. Wheee! hosta has frilly leaves and is smaller overall.

What's that goldfinch doing on your coneflower in fall? It's eating the seeds!

# PURPLE CONEFLOWER

## PROFILE

If there's one perennial in this whole chapter that you need to plant, then this is it. (Wait, did I say that already?) Seriously, this is the one. Purple coneflower is so strong, comes back year after year, and adds fantastic color in the garden. Butterflies adore it. Butterflies love it. And the color is spectacular. It truly aims to please and even offers great visual interest if you keep the plant up throughout winter.

## STATS

| Common Name | Coneflower, purple coneflower |
|---|---|
| Botanical Name | *Echinacea purpurea* |
| Zone | 4 to 9 |
| Height | 1½ to 4 feet |
| Spread | 1 to 2 feet |
| Flower Color | Purplish pink, though new cultivars also come in red, magenta, orange, yellow, green, and more |
| Light Needs | Full sun to part shade |

## 🌣 GREEN THUMB TIP

There are so many amazing coneflowers available that are *gorgeous*. If you fall in love with some of these, you just need to keep one thing in mind: these newer varieties might not last as long. Don't let this deter you from planting them, though. But if you're looking for ones that last for years, stick to the natives or consult your local garden center.

## ✓ TOP PICKS

Here are some of the cool new options you can find on the market today: Green Envy offers green blooms that turn pink as they age. Butterfly Kisses or Double Scoop Raspberry are both double bloomers. Lemon Yellow or Cleopatra are good options if you want yellow. Tangerine Dream is deep orange. Sombrero Salsa Red is deep red and gorgeous!

# GOLDENROD

## PROFILE

Gardeners often overlook goldenrod because it doesn't necessarily have big or showy flowers. It's mostly known as a wildflower, growing wild in meadows, fields, and parks. It does have some superior qualities, though. For instance, it's drought-tolerant and can grow in a wide range of conditions. The flowers bloom in late summer and then last all the way through fall. It's starting to make a bit of a comeback because it's so popular among bees and butterflies.

## STATS

| Common Name | Goldenrod |
|---|---|
| Botanical Name | *Solidago speciosa* |
| Zone | 3 to 8 |
| Height | 2 to 3 feet |
| Spread | 2 to 3 feet |
| Flower Color | Yellow |
| Light Needs | Full sun |

## GREEN THUMB TIP

Plant two or three of these in the front of your perennial border. They'll add a great splash of yellow, yet they are short enough not to overshadow other plants.

# YUCCA

## PROFILE

Planting yucca will save you a little taste of the desert. It does well in poor or sandy soils, and it is definitely eye-catching growing in the garden. It has spiky green foliage that looks like it could be growing in the Southwest. Then in the summer, it will send off tall stalks of gorgeous, bell-shaped white flowers, several feet into the air. Even after the blooms fade, you'll still have that spiky foliage to add some fun to your garden.

## STATS

| | |
|---|---|
| Common Name | Yucca, Adam's needle, needle plant |
| Botanical Name | *Yucca filamentosa* |
| Zone | 5 to 10 |
| Height | 4 to 8 feet |
| Spread | 2 to 3 feet |
| Flower Color | Grown for its spiky green foliage and also shoots off-white blooms |
| Light Needs | Full sun |

## GREEN THUMB TIP

It says full sun, but surprisingly, it'll do really well in some shady spots, too. Just make sure that it still has some sun throughout the day to establish the plants.

51

Butterflies love black-eyed Susans, so it's not uncommon to see them stopping by for nectar.

# BLACK-EYED SUSAN

## PROFILE

While a lot of perennial flowers do best if they get a head start as plants, black-eyed Susans are a good one to grow from seed if you'd like. They can produce dozens of flowers on a single plant, even crowding out some of your other plants, so position with caution if you're growing these for the first time. They have the signature "black eye" in the center of the flowers with beautiful golden blooms. They will grow best in fertile, well-drained soil, but they're actually pretty forgiving, too, so if you have a challenging soil type, give 'em a try.

## STATS

| Common Name | Black-eyed Susan, rudbeckia |
| --- | --- |
| Botanical Name | *Rudbeckia fulgida* |
| Zone | 3 to 9 |
| Height | 2 to 4 feet |
| Spread | 2 to 3 feet |
| Flower Color | Golden yellow |
| Light Needs | Full sun to part shade |

## ● GREEN THUMB TIP

As your black-eyed Susans start to fade in the summer, cut back the flowers—there's a chance you might encourage them to bloom again in fall.

## ✓ TOP PICKS

Goldstrum is one of the most popular varieties available, and Viette's Little Suzy is a smaller cultivar. Check with your local native plant society for many different types of Rudbeckia.

It's common to see ants crawling around on peony buds before the flowers open.

# GARDEN PEONY

## PROFILE

Hands down, garden peonies have some of the most gorgeous, fragrant flowers in the garden. They are also quite delicate, so if you pick them to put in a vase, you'll probably get only a few days out of them. Peonies (which some people actually throw into the shrub category) are one of the most sought-after blooms because of the great spring color they bring. They've been a favorite among gardeners for generations. Chances are good that your grandmother had peonies growing in her yard (and maybe still does). One of the best things about them is that once they are established, they can live up to one hundred years.

## STATS

| Common Name | Garden peonies |
| --- | --- |
| Botanical Name | *Paeonia* |
| Zone | 3 to 8 |
| Height | 2 to 3 feet |
| Spread | 2 to 3 feet |
| Flower Color | Golden yellow |
| Light Needs | Full sun to part shade |

## 🌀 GREEN THUMB TIP

For the most part, peonies are pretty maintenance-free; however, their big heavy blooms do cause them to droop. For this reason, you'll want to plant them in a more protected area, out of the wind. Some people even stake their peonies so the blooms don't cause the branches to fall to the ground.

## TOP PICKS

For early flowers, look for Early Scout. Firelight has gorgeous, pale pink flowers. Elsa Sassflowers are great later in the spring and feature white blooms. Heirloom peonies are popular and have fantastic fragrance. New peony varieties are often more compact and hold up better, but keep in mind you might lose some of that fragrance.

# COREOPSIS

## PROFILE

Heat, humidity, and drought are no competition for coreopsis. Neither is poor soil. Coreopsis will do great in just about any condition. Of course, this can be a good or bad thing, depending on how you look at it. It's common to see this plant growing as a wildflower out in meadows and fields. It's not a super tall plant, but it really adds great shades of sunshine in any garden.

## STATS

| | |
|---|---|
| Common Name | Coreopsis |
| Botanical Name | *Coreopsis* |
| Zone | 4 to 9 |
| Height | 6 inches to 3 feet |
| Spread | 1 to 2 feet |
| Flower Color | Yellow but newer varieties are red, white, and bicolor |
| Light Needs | Full sun |

### GREEN THUMB TIP

If you want to encourage the plants to rebloom, trim back a bit in mid to late summer.

### ✓ TOP PICKS

Double Sunburst has double blooms that are extremely striking in the garden. Baby Gold is a tried-and-true favorite.

# BLANKET FLOWER

## PROFILE

Blanket flower earned its name because it resembles blankets woven by Native Americans. This perennial is a little on the short side, so it's the perfect perennial to plant at the front border of your garden. The flowers are striking with multiple colors of red, orange, and yellow. They demand well-drained soil. You can try starting this one from seed, but if they don't take, opt for a plant from the garden center instead. This flower is also a favorite of bees.

## STATS

| | |
|---|---|
| Common Name | Blanket flower |
| Botanical Name | *Gaillardia × grandiflora* |
| Zone | 3 to 10 |
| Height | 8 inches to 2 feet |
| Spread | 1 to 2 feet |
| Flower Color | Mixture of yellow, orange, and red |
| Light Needs | Full sun |

## 🌱 GREEN THUMB TIP

Generally, this plant doesn't need to be deadheaded at all; however, if you remove the spent blooms toward the end of summer, you just might encourage them to rebloom in the fall. Keep in mind, this plant is pretty short-lived, so if you notice it fading after a couple years, plant more!

# BUTTERFLY WEED

Many don't realize it, but butterfly weed is actually in the milkweed family, so it counts as a host plant for monarchs. More than monarchs love it—plenty of other butterflies will stop by to enjoy its nectar, too. Butterfly weed is a native perennial that does really well in all types of soil, and it's known by gardeners to be drought-tolerant.

## STATS

| Common Name | Butterfly weed |
|---|---|
| Botanical Name | *Asclepias tuberosa* |
| Zone | 3 to 9 |
| Height | 2 to 3 feet |
| Spread | 1 to 2 feet |
| Flower Color | Orange |
| Light Needs | Full sun |

## 🌰 GREEN THUMB TIP

You can grow butterfly weed from seed, but it's not always easy to find. Instead, opt for plants and you'll see blooms that same summer.

# SHASTA DAISY

## PROFILE

Have you ever seen daisies growing alongside the road or in a field? Shasta daisies are very similar, but the backyard variety has more and bigger blooms. Still, they are the classic daisy flower, and the bright white blooms are sure to brighten up a garden. If you plant by seed, it'll take a couple seasons before they produce in full. Otherwise, look for plants at your local garden center. Divide the plants every few years to keep them producing at top capacity.

## STATS

| | |
|---|---|
| Common Name | Shasta daisy |
| Botanical Name | *Leucanthemum × superbum* |
| Zone | 5 to 9 |
| Height | 1 to 4 feet |
| Spread | 1 to 3 feet |
| Flower Color | White |
| Light Needs | Full sun |

## 🔍 GREEN THUMB TIP

When trying to get Shasta daisies established, be sure to plant them in well-drained soil and give them lots of water. They are a pretty low-maintenance plant overall, but this will help early on. Then you'll have years of flowers!

## ✓ TOP PICKS

Snow Lady is actually a Shasta daisy that you can get to flower from seed in its first year. Daisy May reblooms several times. Highland White Dream is a great tall variety with large flowers.

Yes, cats love this plant. So snip off a few pieces to bring inside to your cat.

# CATMINT

## PROFILE

Gardeners grow catmint for the foliage (silvery green leaves) as much as they do for the blooms. This is seriously one resilient perennial. If you're looking for something to fill space, this is a great candidate because it's really full as it spreads out. Some gardeners say that it's deer-resistant, so if you have that problem, it's worth a shot. Plant catmint a few feet apart and then watch it thrive. You don't have to water it much, either. This is a great plant for feeding the bees! Butterflies and hummingbirds like it, too.

## STATS

| | |
|---|---|
| Common Name | Catmint |
| Botanical Name | *Nepeta* |
| Zone | 3 to 8 |
| Height | 1 to 3 feet |
| Spread | 1 to 4 feet |
| Flower Color | Periwinkle blue, purple |
| Light Needs | Full sun |

### GREEN THUMB TIP

This plant is an early bloomer and will produce flowers by late spring. As it starts to fade in summer, cut it back by about one-third and you'll likely be rewarded with new growth and blooms for late summer and fall.

### ✓ TOP PICKS

You can find tons of great catmint varieties today: Walker's Low earned the honor of Perennial Plant of the Year in 2007. Little Titch is a dwarf kind that grows less than a foot tall. Blue Wonder has beautiful blue flowers. Purrsian Blue is a vigorous grower that stays neatly compact all season (14 to 18 inches) without the need for trimming.

# TALL GARDEN PHLOX

## PROFILE

Phlox is widely known and grown in the gardening world. You can find creeping phlox, which many use as a groundcover or filler plant in their perennial bed, but let's take a look at the tall and beloved tall garden phlox. You can find this flower in gardens as well as growing in the wild with tons of beautiful blooms on each stalk. If you grow it in your garden, you can expect to have months of great color and butterflies, too. It's really one of the longest blooming perennials in the garden.

## STATS

| | |
|---|---|
| Common Name | Phlox, tall garden phlox |
| Botanical Name | *Phlox paniculata* |
| Zone | 4 to 8 |
| Height | 15 inches to 4 feet |
| Spread | 1½ to 3 feet |
| Flower Color | Pink, purple, red, coral, white, bicolor |
| Light Needs | Full sun to part shade |

## GREEN THUMB TIP

Sometimes phlox has the reputation of being susceptible to the plant disease known as powdery mildew. So look for newer varieties that have been grown to be mildew-resistant.

# YARROW

## PROFILE

Yarrow is one perennial plant that sometimes get a bad reputation because they easily spread. (This is because they have rhizomes, which send off lateral shoots.) Not all varieties are so aggressive, though, so if you don't mind how quickly they could spread, definitely try this plant in your garden. It's one of the most drought-tolerant options you can grow. While other plants will fade in the hot, humid, dry summer, it will keep right on growing and looking great with its tiny little flowers.

## STATS

| Common Name | Yarrow |
|---|---|
| Botanical Name | *Achillea millefolium* |
| Zone | 3 to 8 |
| Height | 1 to 3 feet |
| Spread | 1 to 3 feet |
| Flower Color | White, yellow, pink, red, and purple |
| Light Needs | Full sun |

## 🌿 GREEN THUMB TIP

Yarrow is traditionally white or sometimes yellow. Look for the newer colors of yarrow, which have beautiful color and are more well-behaved in the garden. (They're still drought-tolerant.)

This plant is available in every color of the rainbow except blue.

# CORAL BELLS

Think of coral bells as being similar to (some might say cooler than) hostas. While they won't take quite as much shade as hostas, many gardeners love them for similar reasons. They are very shade-tolerant (but do well in sun, too), and if you like plants with nice foliage, you can get them in a huge range of options. Seriously, you can get plants with leaves that are orange, black, purple, red, green, silver, and yellow. While they aren't known for their flowers, some varieties do have colorful blooms. They typically bloom in late spring to early summer, and hummingbirds love them.

## STATS

| Common Name | Coral bells |
|---|---|
| Botanical Name | *Heuchera* |
| Zone | 4 to 9 |
| Height | 1 to 3 feet |
| Spread | 1 to 2 feet |
| Flower Color | Grown for foliage, in a huge array of colors, including orange, black, purple, red, green, silver, and yellow |
| Light Needs | Full sun to full shade |

## GREEN THUMB TIP

When researching this plant and figuring out what you want to grow, be sure to use the botanical name—*Heuchera*—because many people know the plant as this.

## ✓ TOP PICKS

Blackberry Ice has vibrant purple foliage. Berry Smoothie has rose purple foliage and beautiful pink flowers. Citronelle is bright lime green to yellow. Caramel is golden orange. Berry Timeless is green with pink flowers. Fire Alarm is bright and beautiful!

Try growing sedum in your containers. It adds some cool texture.

# SEDUM

## PROFILE

As part of the succulent family, sedum is easy to grow, doesn't require a lot of water, and once you get it established, it can last for years. This perennial (most people know it as autumn stonecrop) has thick stems and leaves, and tiny star-shaped flowers that really pack a punch when you grow two or three plants together. If you have a really dry area or a rock garden, then you'll definitely want to check out sedum because it might be one of the only things you can get to thrive there.

## STATS

| | |
|---|---|
| Common Name | Sedum, stonecrop, autumn stonecrop |
| Botanical Name | *Sedum* |
| Zone | 4 to 9 |
| Height | 3 inches to 3 feet |
| Spread | 1 to 3 feet |
| Flower Color | Pink, magenta, red, white, yellow |
| Light Needs | Full sun |

## 🌀 GREEN THUMB TIP

Autumn stonecrop offers good foliage early on in the season, but it really comes alive in late summer and fall when the weather starts to get cooler. This is when the flowers really turn bright and beautiful. So if it doesn't seem like your sedum is doing everything it should right away, just have a little patience.

## ✓ TOP PICKS

You can get so many different types of sedum. Look for the cultivar Fulda Glow or Lime Zinger, both rich in color. Also look for the cultivar called Brilliant (*Sedum spectabile),* which is a beautiful bright pink.

# TRUMPET VINE

## PROFILE

Trumpet vine is one of the biggest, most striking, awesome hummingbird plants you can grow. Once you get it established, it loyally comes back every year, growing 20, 30, and even 40 feet, attracting hummingbirds the entire season. The trumpet-shaped flowers are gorgeous and bright. They will attract butterflies and bees. You definitely need a strong support system to grow this vine—an old stump, sturdy pergola, even a telephone pole. It's truly one of the most eye-catching plants in the garden.

## STATS

| | |
|---|---|
| Common Name | Trumpet vine, trumpet creeper |
| Botanical Name | *Campsis radicans* |
| Zone | 4 to 9 |
| Height | 10 to 40 feet |
| Spread | 5 to 20 feet |
| Flower Color | Orange, scarlet, or yellow |
| Light Needs | Full sun to partial shade |

## 🖐 GREEN THUMB TIP

This plant has suckers, so this means it sends off lots of offshoots to grow. Some even consider it aggressive or invasive, so don't get it started if you don't have the space and support. But otherwise, it's one of the best vines you can select.

# FAQS ON PERENNIALS

### Do perennials really come back every year?

Yes. Well, kinda. Well, mostly. Perennials do come back year after year, but they aren't miracle plants. Eventually, most perennials will likely die, either because of a harsh winter, overcrowding, or other reasons. In general, you can find both short-lived and long-lived perennials. Don't let this deter you, though. One of the best things about perennials is that they are a great investment because you'll get many years out of them.

### What about new varieties of perennials that I hear about?

They are great! In many instances, they live longer than the originals. (This isn't always the case, though. Coneflowers and tulips are both examples where they don't last as long.) In general, newer varieties are better adapted to today's garden, and they have fewer problems with things like disease. If you're not sure, just ask. Chances are, the experts at your local garden center know exactly why a new variety is cool or unique.

### Where's the best place to buy perennials?

Your local garden center should have an excellent selection of perennials. However, if you're looking for newer varieties, natives, heirlooms, etc., then you might want to take your search online. If you saw some of the "top picks" in this chapter that you want to try, do an online search for them.

### How many perennials are there?

You can seriously find thousands of varieties of perennials out there. This chapter was hard to write because how do you select *the best* perennials when there are so many options?! Here's a tip—if you see something you like in a friend or neighbor's garden, find out what it is. Just ask, because gardeners are often happy to tell you. They're usually proud of their plants. This is how to figure out what you like most.

### What's the best benefit of perennials?

Hands down, they're a great investment. In many instances, you'll want to buy plants (versus seeds) or the perennial you want might only be available in a plant. This could mean a slightly larger initial investment from you, but they'll be reliable for years!

# GRASSES

A chapter on growing grass?! Don't you just throw out some seed and call it a day? No, no, no—there's more to it than that. And there are many, many more grasses in the world than the green blades you find in golf courses, parks, and backyards. When you learn about the appeal of a wonderful group of plants called ornamental grasses, then you can add all kinds of beauty to your backyard. Gardeners grow grasses for their foliage instead of their flowers. They can add great texture and gorgeous color to your yard, especially in fall. Plus, they are like secret weapons when it comes to attracting birds and butterflies.

Fountain grass gets its name because it looks like a fountain spewing water.

# FOUNTAIN GRASS

Like many ornamental grasses, fountain grass can provide great visual interest long after summer. The foliage changes to a beautiful golden color in fall, and then it fades to a beige in winter where you can leave it up all season to add texture to the garden. If grown in the right conditions (good sun without too much shade), you can get this grass to flower. Look for small, silvery–pink blooms in mid to late summer.

## STATS

| Common Name | Fountain grass |
|---|---|
| Botanical Name | *Pennisetum alopecuroides* |
| Zone | 6 to 9 |
| Height | up to 5 feet |
| Spread | up to 5 feet |
| Foliage | Green with some gold fall color |
| Light Needs | Full sun to part shade |

## GREEN THUMB TIP

This grass is one of the most versatile out there. Put it along borders or in containers. It also has few to no problems with diseases, so it's a sure thing!

# BLUE FESCUE

## PROFILE

It might be one of the smallest grasses available, but it's also one of the most interesting in color with its spiky blades that have a silvery blue hue. The dome shape of this plant almost looks like a porcupine, hiding among the other perennials in your flowerbed. This one can take some shade. In fact, if you have extremely hot or dry summers, it's probably a good idea to place it in shade so it won't die off in the heat.

## STATS

| | |
|---|---|
| Common Name | Blue fescue |
| Botanical Name | *Festuca glauca* |
| Zone | 4 to 8 |
| Height | up to 1 foot |
| Spread | up to 1½ feet |
| Foliage | Green with a bluish or purplish tinge |
| Light Needs | Full sun to part shade |

### 🌿 GREEN THUMB TIP

Group several blue fescues together along the front of a flowerbed to make an attractive and unique border. Also, it's best to divide this grass every few years to keep it growing healthy.

### ✓ TOP PICKS

One of the most popular and trouble-free options when it comes to blue fescue is a variety called Elijah Blue.

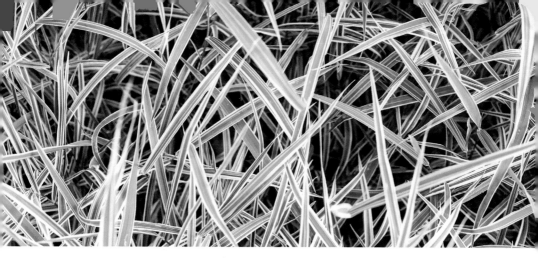

# SEDGE

## PROFILE

Everyone has that space in their garden where they can't seem to get anything to grow. Try this grass—it can grow in a variety of conditions, including sun and shade. Plus, it works in a lot of different soil types. This grass spreads by rhizomes under the ground, so in just a few years, a couple of plants could double or triple. This makes them a great candidate when you're looking for a groundcover.

## STATS

| | |
|---|---|
| Common Name | Sedge, carex |
| Botanical Name | *Carex* |
| Zone | 4 to 8 |
| Height | up to 1½ feet |
| Spread | up to 1½ feet |
| Foliage | Green or green and yellow |
| Light Needs | Sun or shade |

## 🌿 GREEN THUMB TIP

This plant usually keeps its shape and at least some of its color year-round. So no matter the time of year, it'll add beauty to your garden.

Plant Karl Foerster behind coneflowers or daisies for a great look all summer.

# FEATHER REED GRASS

## PROFILE

You can find plants known as reed grass and also as feather reed grass, but one of the most popular to look for is the Karl Foerster variety. This is the one that gardeners seem to love most. It actually won the Perennial Plant of the Year honor in 2001. Whether you look for this specific one or other feather reed grass, all offer good color and interest in winter. Plus, it's definitely a favorite grass among birds! It has wheat-like seed heads that appear in late spring and go through fall.

## STATS

| Common Name | Feather reed grass, Karl Foerster |
|---|---|
| Botanical Name | *Calamagrostis × acutiflora* |
| Zone | 5 to 9 |
| Height | up to 5 feet |
| Spread | up to 3 feet |
| Foliage | Green with purplish or golden tops |
| Light Needs | Full sun |

## GREEN THUMB TIP

It's no wonder gardeners love this plant. It does well in clay soil, and it can even take some shade in warm climates.

## GARDEN HISTORY

This plant was named after—you guessed it—a German plant guy named Karl Foerster. He introduced it in a book in the 1950s, and it made its way to the United States in the 1960s.

# NORTHERN SEA OATS

## PROFILE

Love grasses but have a ton of shade? This one might be just what you're looking for! Northern sea oats is one of the most shade-tolerant grasses available. So if you have an area that doesn't see much sun, give it a try. It has these flat, drooping seedheads that start off green and then take on purple and golden hues by the end of summer. It can be a little aggressive overall, often reseeding and producing plants on its own. This can be a good or bad thing, depending on your perspective—or where you want to plant it.

## STATS

| Common Name | Northern sea oats, inland sea oats |
| --- | --- |
| Botanical Name | *Chasmanthium latifolium* |
| Zone | 3 to 8 |
| Height | up to 5 feet |
| Spread | up to 3 feet |
| Foliage | Green to straw gold |
| Light Needs | Full sun to part shade |

## GREEN THUMB TIP

Definitely leave this grass up for winter. Don't cut it back until spring. Not only will this make your garden more interesting during the cold months, but it'll help keep this plant protected.

# MAIDEN GRASS

## PROFILE

This is one tough grass. It thrives in a variety of soils, including sandy and clay. It also does pretty well in many light conditions, though it tends to flop a bit if it gets too much shade. It starts out green and then brightens to a nice golden shade in fall before fading to beige for winter. It tends to be a late bloomer—look for crimson flowers late in summer or early fall.

## STATS

| | |
|---|---|
| Common Name | Maiden grass, eulalia |
| Botanical Name | *Miscanthus sinensis* 'Gracillimus' |
| Zone | 5 to 9 |
| Height | up to 7 feet |
| Spread | up to 6 feet |
| Foliage | Green to gold and beige |
| Light Needs | Full sun to part shade |

## 🍃 GREEN THUMB TIP

You can create an excellent fall display with this grass. Just cut off large stalks of it and tie it with string. Pair it with some dried corn on your porch, and your decorating is done.

Share zebra grass with friends by dividing the whole clump in spring.

# ZEBRA GRASS

You definitely won't mistake zebra grass from another type of grass; it has very distinct striping all up and down the blades, which give it its name. It's also a grass that can take a wide range of soil types, including sandy and clay. (Are you starting to become a fan of grasses yet? They're so forgiving!) Look for showy flowers that peek over the foliage in late summer. This is truly a "plant it and forget it" kind of grass. You should have years of success with it.

## STATS

| Common Name | Zebra grass |
|---|---|
| Botanical Name | *Miscanthus sinensis ‹Zebrinus›* |
| Zone | 5 to 9 |
| Height | up to 8 feet |
| Spread | up to 6 feet |
| Foliage | Green with pale striping |
| Light Needs | Full sun to part shade |

### GREEN THUMB TIP

Some types of *Miscanthus* are considered invasive, so you'll want to stay away from them. Be aware of this if you look to add zebra grass to your garden.

# SWITCH GRASS

You can find many options in the switch grass family—seriously, grass families are huge! For this one, look for cultivars like Cheyenne Sky, Ruby Ribbons, and Prairie Fire. Gardeners grow it because it quickly goes from green to a reddish purple in just a couple short months. Nearly all ornamental grasses change colors in fall, but this one does it much earlier, adding fantastic color in the garden among your flowers.

## STATS

| Common Name | Switch grass |
|---|---|
| Botanical Name | *Panicum virgatum* |
| Zone | 5 to 9 |
| Height | up to 4 feet |
| Spread | up to 4 feet |
| Foliage | Green and then burgundy |
| Light Needs | Full sun |

## GREEN THUMB TIP

It's so low-maintenance—this native grass will grow in any soil, from sand to clay. It's also drought-tolerant, and once you have it established, it'll even withstand periodic flooding.

# FAQS ON GRASSES

## What's an ornamental grass?

These are arguably the coolest, most underrated plants in the gardening world. Grasses are meant to grow tall and give great color, texture, and interest to your yard.

## How's it different than the grass in my lawn?

It's not even close to being the same. To be honest, lawn grass has very little benefit, other than looking green. Ornamental grasses, on the other hands, have tons of benefits. For example, they're often good plants for butterflies, birds, bees, good insects, etc.

## How are grasses different from perennials?

Actually, many ornamental grasses *are* perennials since they come back year after year. So they can be very similar, and you might see them grouped together at your local garden center or if you're shopping online.

## Why would anyone want to grow grass?

Not only do they have great benefits for wildlife, but they are also great fillers! This means they grow big and tall and wide (not all, but many), making them excellent candidates for when you need to fill a space. Plus, they give great winter interest, are easy to grow, and are low to no maintenance!

# SHRUBS & TREES

Let's be honest for a minute. You likely have a big blank space or hole in your yard that you want filled as soon as possible. This is why you're in the tree and shrub chapter, right? Never fear because these are some of the most reliable, sure-thing plants available at garden centers today. They will help your empty space look like a gardener has been working on it for years!

Red twig dogwood has fantastic color in winter, good blooms in spring, and fruit for the birds.

# RED TWIG DOGWOOD

## PROFILE

Dogwoods are some of the best trees and shrubs around (yes, they are considered both trees and shrubs, depending on the variety). Although you can choose from literally hundreds, red twig dogwood is one of the best! You can grow it as a small tree or as a shrub, pruning it as you see fit. This shrub's bright red stems look fantastic in winter when there's not much other color. Looking for a good shrub border for your driveway or between the neighbors? This one is it because of its year-round appeal!

## STATS

| | |
|---|---|
| Common Name | Red twig dogwood, red osier dogwood |
| Botanical Name | *Cornus sericea* |
| Zone | 3 to 7 |
| Height | up to 10 feet |
| Spread | up to 10 feet |
| Foliage | Green leaves and red bark |
| Flower Color | White |
| Light Needs | Full sun to part shade |

## 🌑 GREEN THUMB TIP

You can leave your dogwood alone and it'll do just fine. But if you want the best color each year, remove about 25 percent of the oldest stems, which turn gray as they mature, in early spring.

## ✓ TOP PICKS

A newer option on the market today has yellow stems, which looks great in the garden, too. Look for the botanical name *Cornus sericea* "Flaviramia."

# CRAPEMYRTLE

## PROFILE

Bees adore it . . . butterflies love it . . . and it's a staple in the south. This shrub (which can grow so tall that some mistake it for a tree) is a true sign of spring with its beautiful pink flowers. It can tolerate less-than-perfect soil conditions, and it's common to see rows of these growing in public gardens or bordering long driveways. Sorry northern gardeners, but it might be off limits to you. If you're right on the edge of its hardiness zone, you can try offering it protection over the winter, and you just might get it to grow!

## STATS

| | |
|---|---|
| Common Name | Crapemyrtle |
| Botanical Name | *Lagerstroemia* |
| Zone | 6 to 9 |
| Height | varies between a few feet to 15 plus |
| Spread | a few feet to 12 plus |
| Foliage | Green leaves |
| Flower Color | All shades of pink, red, lavender, and white |
| Light Needs | Full sun |

## 🌑 GREEN THUMB TIP

Crapemyrtle can sometimes have a reputation for being susceptible to plant diseases. Don't worry—newer cultivars have been bred to be disease-resistant, so ask your local garden center or look for options like Comanche or Choctaw. Another option is Chickasaw, which only reaches a few feet tall. The Black Diamond series is also popular.

# WHITE OAK

## PROFILE

Everyone should plant an oak tree in their lifetime; it's the kind of long-term invest-ment that can live on for hundreds of years. The white oak gets its name because of its ashy–gray bark. Not every oak tree will reach a height of 80 feet, but it does need ample space. In due time, it will provide wonderful shade for picnics, reading, and relaxation.

## STATS

| Common Name | White oak |
|---|---|
| Botanical Name | *Quercus alba* |
| Zone | 3 to 9 |
| Height | up to 80 feet |
| Spread | up to 80 feet |
| Foliage | Leaves start off pinkish in spring then go to dark green |
| Light Needs | Full sun |

## GREEN THUMB TIP

Sure, it might not be the fastest-growing tree, but don't let this deter you. It could be the perfect option for planting at your kids' school or in a public park. Now that's how you pay it forward through gardening!

The more, the better with forsythia. If you group these, they really make an impact!

# FORSYTHIA

## PROFILE

The harbinger of spring—this is how gardeners often refer to forsythia. When it's really early in spring and not much else is blooming, the gorgeous golden flowers emerge and brighten up an entire landscape. This shrub really is one of the first things to flower, and it sure does make an impact. You can find gobs of forsythia options out there, including dwarf varieties only reaching a few feet tall to border forsythia, which spreads and is used for borders, hedges, and screening. After the initial bloom, they mostly fade away and are forgotten, but they can still offer a solid swath of green for the rest of the growing season.

## STATS

| Common Name | Forsythia |
|---|---|
| Botanical Name | *Forsythia × intermedia* |
| Zone | 5 to 8 |
| Height | most up to 6 to 8 feet |
| Spread | most up to 6 feet |
| Foliage | Green leaves |
| Flower Color | Bright yellow flowers in spring |
| Light Needs | Full sun to part shade |

### 🌸 GREEN THUMB TIP

You can try to start your own forsythia shrub by taking a stem cutting from an existing plant.

### ✓ TOP PICKS

Sunrise is a cultivar that thrives in colder temperatures. Gold Tide only grows a couple feet tall but can spread up to 4 feet wide. Also ask your local garden center because they might know what will do best in your area.

### ➤➤ GARDEN HISTORY

This plant was named after William Forsyth. He was a Scottish botanist and also helped start the original Royal Horticultural Society.

One hydrangea different from the bigleaf variety that is worth growing is oakleaf hydrangea (*Hydrangea quercifolia*). It has really cool leaves like you'd see on oak trees.

# HYDRANGEA

The world of hydrangeas is *huge!* You can find hundreds and hundreds to choose from, and the botanical names can get a bit confusing. So let's make things simple and focus on one of the most popular, the bigleaf hydrangea. You can find two main groups, including those with globe-shaped flowers (called mopheads) and flattened flower heads (called lacecaps). Both are beautiful, and once you get them established, they grow for years! Don't lose patience if you don't get yours going right away. Sometimes you just need to find the right location in your garden.

## STATS

| Common Name | Hydrangea, bigleaf hydrangea |
|---|---|
| Botanical Name | *Hydrangea macrophylla* |
| Zone | 5 to 9 |
| Height | up to 6 feet |
| Spread | up to 10 feet |
| Foliage | Green |
| Flower Color | Blue, pink, purple, red, white |
| Light Needs | Full sun to part shade |

## ◉ GREEN THUMB TIP

In cold climates, the wind and frigid temperatures can really take a toll on hydrangeas. To protect your investment, cover your plants in winter with burlap or shredded leaves.

## ✓ TOP PICKS

Some varieties like Endless Summer have been developed to rebloom throughout the growing season. You can also get blue and pink cultivars, which is a nice alternative to the traditional white you're probably used to seeing.

# JUNIPER

## PROFILE

The hardest thing to do is figure out whether juniper is a tree or a shrub. The short answer is that it's both! You've probably seen junipers growing before, most of which fall under the botanical name *Juniperus chinensis*. This evergreen is so versatile, and it's very popular for people wanting something to offer a little privacy in the backyard. All junipers are reliable and fairly maintenance-free, though, so you can plant them without worrying. Plus, nearly all produce blue little berries for the birds!

## STATS

| Common Name | Juniper |
|---|---|
| Botanical Name | *Juniperus* |
| Zone | 2 to 9 |
| Height | Greatly varies, up to 50 feet |
| Spread | A few feet to 30-plus feet wide |
| Foliage | Evergreen with an often bluish tinge that offers year-round interest |
| Light Needs | Full sun |

## 🌱 GREEN THUMB TIP

Read plant labels! Since juniper is one of those that can be a few feet high to more than 40 feet tall, make sure you know this before you plant. Remember—you want to know what size it will be at maturity. Just because something is small when you buy it in the garden center doesn't mean it will stay small!

# RIVER BIRCH

## PROFILE

You've probably heard of paper birch before—it has white papery bark that looks like it's peeling. Well, river birch is a close cousin much better suited for many backyards in the country. The bark alone is enough for most people, but it's also popular because it grows pretty fast. River birch will take a wide range of soil types but is happiest in consistently moist soil. And while many birch trees tend to have trouble with disease, this one usually thrives. Look for the Heritage cultivar.

## STATS

| Common Name | River birch |
|---|---|
| Botanical Name | *Betula nigra* |
| Zone | 4 to 9 |
| Height | up to 70 feet |
| Spread | up to 60 feet |
| Foliage | Green leaves turn yellow in fall |
| Light Needs | Full sun to part shade |

## 🌿 GREEN THUMB TIP

Be sure to keep the root system cool and moist, especially as you're getting this one established.

# RED MAPLE

## PROFILE

Red is definitely in the name of this maple tree for a reason. Before the leaves bud out in spring, many people don't even notice its little red flowers. The tree also features red fruit and reddish stems. Plus, you can't forget its famous red leaves in fall! In general, all maples are good candidates when you're looking to add a tree to your backyard, and this one is one of the best. It grows fairly fast and requires little to no care from you.

## STATS

| Common Name | Red maple |
|---|---|
| Botanical Name | *Acer rubrum* |
| Zone | 3 to 9 |
| Height | up to 70 feet |
| Spread | up to 50 feet |
| Foliage | Green leaves that turn red in fall |
| Light Needs | Full sun |

## GREEN THUMB TIP

Sometimes the roots on this tree are shallow, so keep this in mind if you're going to plant it near a driveway or sidewalk.

# YEW

## PROFILE

Yews are one of the longest-living evergreens and a staple in many backyards. You've probably seen a yew, even if you didn't know what it was. While the entire yew family (*Taxus*) is huge, let's focus on *Taxus × media*. This is a hybrid group made up of English yews, which are great ornamentals, mixed with Japanese yews, which can survive harsh winters. All are good options for getting some year-round green added to your yard, but this group of hybrids is particularly known for being relatively disease-free and easy to care for.

## STATS

| Common Name | Yew |
| --- | --- |
| Botanical Name | *Taxus × media* |
| Zone | 4 to 7 |
| Height | up to 20 feet |
| Spread | up to 12 feet |
| Foliage | Evergreen foliage |
| Light Needs | Full sun to full shade |

## 🌀 GREEN THUMB TIP

The yew is pretty forgiving when it comes to pruning and shaping however you please. You'll want to do this in early spring before new growth has really started. Plus, it's one of the few shrubs that will thrive in full shade!

If the birds don't eat them all, you can actually eat serviceberries yourself. They taste a lot like blueberries.

# SERVICEBERRY

## PROFILE

Here's another one—is it a tree? Is it a shrub? Ask two different gardeners, and you'll get two different answers. And they'd both be right. Think about what's most important to you. Is it fall color? Is it offering food for birds? Is it spring flowers? All serviceberries do this, but some have higher marks than others. For a smaller serviceberry, look for the botanical name *Amelanchier alnifolia*. For a tree, look for botanical names *Amelanchier arborea* and *Amelanchier canadensis*. Once you figure out your number-one priority and you know your space needs, then set out to talk to someone at your local garden center to find a serviceberry that fits those needs.

## STATS

| Common Name | Serviceberry |
|---|---|
| Botanical Name | *Amelanchier* |
| Zone | 3 to 9, depending on species, check the label |
| Height | up to 30 feet |
| Spread | up to 20 feet |
| Foliage | Green, changing to yellow, orange, and red in fall |
| Flower Color | White |
| Light Needs | Full sun to part shade |

## GREEN THUMB TIP

Serviceberry offers excellent berries for birds! Expect to attract robins, waxwings, cardinals, grosbeaks, tanagers, and more.

## ✓ TOP PICKS

Regent is a shrub, and many gardeners grow it for the fruit to make serviceberry jam. Autumn Brilliance is grown as a tree and known for its gorgeous fall color. Princess Diana is known for its yellow flower buds, which open to white flowers.

# ROSE OF SHARON

## PROFILE

Don't be fooled by the name on this one—it's not actually in the rose family at all. Instead, it's related to hibiscus, which generally have tropical-like flowers. Still, gardeners definitely grow it for its blooms, which last all summer. The blooms look a bit like hollyhock, and the shrub is very forgiving overall. In fact, some gardeners love the challenge of training rose of Sharon, pruning it to look like a miniature tree.

## STATS

| | |
|---|---|
| Common Name | Rose of Sharon, shrub althea |
| Botanical Name | *Hibiscus syriacus* |
| Zone | 5 to 8 |
| Height | up to 12 feet |
| Spread | up to 10 feet |
| Foliage | Green |
| Flower Color | Pink, lavender, blue, white, and bicolor |
| Light Needs | Full sun to part shade |

## 🌿 GREEN THUMB TIP

While it will tolerate some shade, you're going to get the best blooms if it gets plenty of sun. Some of these plants will aggressively reseed. Look for seedless cultivars if this is something you're concerned about.

# SPIREA

## PROFILE

Spirea can come in many shapes and sizes. For instance, there's a kind of spirea called bridal wreath (*Spirea vanhouttei*) that can grow 10 feet tall and a whopping 20 feet wide! Because there are so many different types, it's really important to read labels when you're shopping at the garden center. Look at the size listed before you buy. All spireas make great hiding spots and nesting spots for birds. And they are known for producing beautiful spring and summer flowers, too.

## STATS

| | |
|---|---|
| Common Name | Spirea |
| Botanical Name | *Spiraea* |
| Zone | 3 to 8 |
| Height | most up to 10 feet |
| Spread | most up to 8 feet |
| Foliage | Green leaves |
| Flower Color | Pink, red, white, yellow |
| Light Needs | Full sun to part shade |

## 🌿 GREEN THUMB TIP

Spirea is very forgiving to pruning shears, so if yours tends to get out of hand, then start cutting and trimming. It usually bounces back in no time, so you can make it fit the space that you need.

Viburnums are actually closely related to honeysuckle.

# VIBURNUM

Viburnums can vary a lot in size and shape, but they do share a few key important traits. For instance, all viburnums have year-round appeal with flowers in spring, great foliage in summer, nice color in fall, and berries that last through winter. Birders and gardeners like viburnum equally because of the wide appeal it has with birds. If you only have space for a few shrubs in your backyard, definitely make room for a viburnum. There are seriously hundreds to choose from, so you're bound to find one that works in your space. Plus, many on the market today are native cultivars—definitely a bonus!

## STATS

| Common Name | Viburnum |
|---|---|
| Botanical Name | *Viburnum* |
| Zone | 3 to 9, varies by species, read the label |
| Height | up to 15 feet |
| Spread | up to 12 feet |
| Foliage | Green leaves |
| Flower Color | White |
| Light Needs | Full sun to part shade |

## GREEN THUMB TIP

You really don't have to worry about disease issues when you grow viburnum! Make sure you get it established by giving it lots of water in the first year and you'll be set for years.

## ✓ TOP PICKS

Not all viburnum blooms are fragrant, but some really smell great, attracting birds, bees, and butterflies. Try the Koreanspice viburnum (*Viburnum carlesii*). Another fragrant one with big white blooms is the snowball virburnum (*Viburnum × carlcephalum*). For those of you in cold climates, arrowwood viburnums (*Viburnum dentatum*) are very hardy.

# RED OAK

## PROFILE

As far as oak trees go, red oak is one of the faster growing varieties out there. If you're trying to fill a blank space in the backyard quickly, this is a good candidate. If you have sandy soil at all, then you're in luck because this tree actually prefers it to be a bit sandy. Oaks are one of those staple trees that everyone needs to plant at least once in their lifetime. The gorgeous burgundy leaves you'll get in fall makes this one a top choice.

## STATS

| | |
|---|---|
| Common Name | Red oak, northern red oak |
| Botanical Name | *Quercus rubra* |
| Zone | 4 to 8 |
| Height | up to 75 feet |
| Spread | up to 75 feet |
| Foliage | Green leaves change to red or brownish red in fall |
| Light Needs | Full sun |

## GREEN THUMB TIP

Acorns are a nice side benefit to oak trees, but you need to have a little bit of patience. It can take forty years or more for a tree to finally produce acorns.

# FAQS ON TREES & SHRUBS

### Why are trees and shrubs lumped together?

In several instances, large shrubs can be considered trees or small trees can be considered shrubs. All of them have woody growth that remains standing through winter. This is also a group with a huge amount of variety and offerings, so they definitely belong together.

### Are trees and shrubs the best way to fill space in a short amount of time?

It seems like that would be the case, right? The short and ambivalent answer is sometimes. Depending on how big they are when you buy them, trees and shrubs can really do wonders in filling empty spaces. But don't necessarily count on them as being the answer to your empty yard woes. Sometimes perennials, ornamental grasses, or even tall plants like a bed of sunflowers are the way to go!

### Can I get trees that grow really fast?

This is such a common question, and again, the answer is sometimes. But here's a piece of advice—don't just go for the trees that grow fast because you want to fill space. Really take the time to select a tree that is good for your space; you're planting something for the long-term that will live on for many years!

### What are the benefits of shrubs?

Shrubs are great spots for birds to nest. They usually provide a food source, too. Then there are the blooms—many shrubs offer fantastic blooms in the spring or summer. Find the value of shrubs for your yard. You'll be glad you did!

# HOUSEPLANTS

When you're looking to bring a little outside in, then houseplants are the way to go. They can brighten your day, add some nice color, and even improve the air quality in your home. How do you know which ones to grow, though? Start with this list, paying close attention to the light needs listed for each one. If you're trying to put a houseplant where it gets no sunshine whatsoever, then you're going to have to limit your options. But if you have a bright window to set it near, you'll have plenty to choose from. Get your containers ready because these houseplants are definitely the most foolproof!

# RUBBER PLANT

## PROFILE

One of the main issues people have with this plant is watering it too much—which tends to make the leaves fall off. Start with a small rubber plant to sit on your table-top, and then watch it grow several feet over the years. If you need to clean your houseplant's leaves, just lightly wipe them off with a damp sponge.

## STATS

| Common Name | Rubber plant |
|---|---|
| Botanical Name | *Ficus elastica* 'Decora' |
| Height | up to a few feet |
| Foliage | Green leaves but some varieties offer red or purplish foliage |
| Light Needs | Medium |

## GREEN THUMB TIP

This one can be a bit toxic to dogs and cats if they get hold of the leaves. Keep this in mind if you have a curious pet.

DID YOU KNOW, THIS PLANT RELEASES A MILKY SUBSTANCE THAT WAS ONCE USED TO MAKE RUBBER?

# SNAKE PLANT

The name alone is reason enough to grow this classic houseplant—you'll have something to tell your friends when they come over! The most important thing to remember with snake plant is that you should make sure you grow it in the right sized pot. Don't put it in a giant container or confine it in something too small. You want it to be just right, giving it a little space to grow. Once it fills the pot, move one size up.

## STATS

| Common Name | Snake plant, mother-in-law's tongue |
|---|---|
| Botanical Name | *Sansevieria trifasciata* |
| Height | up to 4 feet |
| Spread | up to 2 feet |
| Foliage | Green with stripes and patterns resembling a snake's skin |
| Light Needs | Low |

## 🌀 GREEN THUMB TIP

If your snake plant is getting big, repot it in summer and put it out on your patio in a shady spot. The fresh air will be good for it!

Find a great selection of air plants
at www.airplantsupplyco.com.

# AIR PLANT

If you've never heard of air plant before, get ready to be amazed. This plant is an epiphyte, which means it doesn't need soil at all—yes, this is seriously true! These are the plants you'll see in those floating glass containers or just sitting on top of a bed of feng shui rocks. You can even find them made into necklaces! In fact, searching for containers for air plants is half the fun!

## STATS

| | |
|---|---|
| Common Name | Air plant |
| Botanical Name | *Tillandsia* |
| Height | Most are 4 to 6 inches |
| Spread | 4 to 6 inches |
| Foliage | Spiky green, sometimes shades of red and orange |
| Light Needs | High |

## GREEN THUMB TIP

The care for this plant is so easy; you just mist it a couple of times a week, and it's good to go!

## ✓ TOP PICKS

Add a little color with an air plant that has pink spikes. Look for *Tillandsia aeranthos* "Amethyst."

# BOSTON FERN

## PROFILE

The Boston fern has a reputation for being a little difficult, but that's not actually true—you just have to grow it in the right conditions. These ferns need a cool place with high humidity and indirect light to thrive. High humidity means it's the perfect houseplant for your kitchen or bathroom. It would also be a great candidate for a hanging basket. If you can meet its basic needs, then you'll definitely have success.

## STATS

| Common Name | Boston fern |
|---|---|
| Botanical Name | *Nephrolepis exaltata* |
| Height | up to 3 feet |
| Spread | up to 3 feet |
| Foliage | Green |
| Light Needs | Low |

## 🌼 GREEN THUMB TIP

You're going to want to keep it moist year-round. Often times, houseplants get less water in winter months, but you'll want to keep this one watered consistently. This plant struggles from low humidity in the house during winter—mist indoors during winter.

# CHRISTMAS CACTUS

## PROFILE

This plant is often passed down from one generation to the next. While the plant is known for having beautiful pink, orange, or white blooms around the holidays, many consider it difficult to get to rebloom in the following years. But don't be intimidated. The plant just needs uninterrupted dark periods (about twelve hours each night) to stimulate bud formation. If you start this treatment in fall, you'll have blooms just in time for Christmas. Even if you can't get the blooms going, it still offers great foliage.

## STATS

| Common Name | Christmas cactus |
|---|---|
| Botanical Name | *Schlumbergera × buckleyi* |
| Height | up to a foot |
| Spread | up to 2 feet |
| Foliage | Green, flat leaves |
| Flower Color | Pink, red, coral, white |
| Light Needs | Bright, indirect light |

## 🌑 GREEN THUMB TIP

A common mistake with Christmas cactus is to give it a lot of heat but not a lot of water. Don't do this! Keep it watered and give it lots of light, too.

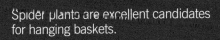
Spider plants are excellent candidates for hanging baskets.

# SPIDER PLANT

## PROFILE

You'll see this plant growing outdoors in warmer climates, but for the rest of the country, it makes a reliable houseplant. It's native to South Africa and is very forgiving if you're the forgetful type when it comes to watering. This is because it has tuberous roots that can store important nutrients for a long time. If the leaf tips start to get brown, though, you should probably add water.

## STATS

| Common Name | Spider plant |
|---|---|
| Botanical Name | *Chlorophytum comosum* |
| Height | up to 2 feet |
| Spread | up to 2 feet |
| Foliage | Green with white stripes around the edges |
| Light Needs | Medium to low light |

## GREEN THUMB TIP

Don't let this plant get too big for the pot it's in. Once you start to see it running out of space, gently break up the roots, separate into several smaller pieces, and repot them into new containers. If you give a couple away, that'll make you a great friend, too!

# DRACAENA

## PROFILE

If you've ever had houseplants, then there's a good chance you've grown a dracaena. In fact, you might not have even known that's what you were growing! Make sure you give this one room because once it gets going, it can eventually reach heights of 10 to 12 feet. These plants with strappy foliage need to have good drainage, but other than that, they're easy.

## STATS

| Common Name | Dracaena |
|---|---|
| Botanical Name | *Dracaena* |
| Height | up to 10 feet |
| Spread | up to 5 feet |
| Foliage | Green with some striping along the edges |
| Light Needs | Medium |

## GREEN THUMB TIP

Sometimes houseplants can be a little finicky when it comes to room temperature. Dracaena is pretty forgiving, but you'll want to make sure it doesn't get too cold.

# ENGISH IVY

Here's another vine that is a staple in the houseplant world. Actually, it's a staple in many gardens, too. It can reach crazy heights of 80 feet in outdoor settings. Indoors, it can trail quite a bit, too, especially if it has something to grow up or around. Inside, it'll be looking for a lot of light. But if you take it outside, it can actually tolerate a lot of shade.

## STATS

| Common Name | English ivy |
| --- | --- |
| Botanical Name | *Hedera helix* |
| Height | up to 10 feet |
| Spread | up to 10 feet |
| Foliage | Green |
| Light Needs | High |

## 🌱 GREEN THUMB TIP

If you have a friend with an English ivy plant, ask if you can take a cutting and try to root it directly into the soil. Not only is this fun, but it's also an inexpensive way to gain a plant.

# JADE PLANT

Jade plant has been around for decades, but you may know it by its other common name: money plant. This shouldn't be confused with the money tree houseplant, which goes by the botanical name of *Pachira aquatica*. The jade plant has thick leaves, and it's great for beginners. It also makes a great gift—many people say it brings luck and wealth.

## STATS

| | |
|---|---|
| Common Name | Jade plant, money plant |
| Botanical Name | *Crassula ovata* |
| Height | up to 3 feet |
| Spread | up to 1 foot |
| Foliage | Green waxy leaves |
| Flower Color | White |
| Light Needs | High to medium |

## GREEN THUMB TIP

Similar to the bonsai and how it looks like a miniature tree, you can train or trim your jade plant to the shape you want.

# GOLDEN POTHOS

## PROFILE

This is a vining plant that truly grows anywhere. It's been around forever and often gets overlooked, but it's so versatile. Plus, you don't have to worry about it getting diseases or having to repot it often. This plant does really well in offices because it doesn't mind (even thrives) on fluorescent light.

## STATS

| Common Name | Pothos |
|---|---|
| Botanical Name | *Epipremnum aureum* |
| Height | trails to 8 feet |
| Spread | trails to 8 feet |
| Foliage | Green |
| Light Needs | Medium |

## 🌿 GREEN THUMB TIP
Because this vining plant can really get growing, you'll want to cut it back a couple times a year to keep it in check and encourage new growth.

DID YOU KNOW POTHOS IS ONE OF THE BEST PLANTS FOR REMOVING FORMALDEHYDE FROM THE AIR OF YOUR HOME?

# WAX PLANT

## PROFILE

This easy-to-grow plant is technically a vine, though it grows quite slowly. It produces clusters of adorable little star-shaped flowers—if you can get it to bloom. (A lot of gardeners don't even realize this plant blooms.) Both the flowers and the leaves are waxy, just as the name implies. You can't go wrong with this one if you're just getting started. You'll have it for years!

## STATS

| | |
|---|---|
| Common Name | Wax plant |
| Botanical Name | *Hoya carnosa* |
| Height | trails up to 10 feet |
| Spread | trails up to 10 feet |
| Foliage | Waxy green |
| Flower Color | White or pink |
| Light Needs | High |

## 🌿 GREEN THUMB TIP

A good rule of thumb is to water your houseplants with room temperature water. You don't want to use really cold water because this can sometimes shock them.

# PEACE LILY

This is one of the most popular plants to give as a gift, and it's also one of the easiest houseplants to grow. It is known for the white "blooms." (They look like flowers but aren't technically flowers at all. Instead, they are called spathes.) The most common mistake with this plant is watering too much, so take it easy. Remember that it's easy to add water, but it's a lot harder to take it away.

## STATS

| Common Name | Peace lily |
|---|---|
| Botanical Name | *Spathiphyllum wallisii* |
| Height | up to 2 feet |
| Spread | up to 2 feet |
| Foliage | Shiny green |
| Flower Color | White |
| Light Needs | Low to moderate |

### GREEN THUMB TIP

Like many houseplants, you don't want to grow this one in direct sunlight. Indirect is always best because then it won't damage the leaves.

# FAQS ON HOUSEPLANTS

### What's the benefit of having houseplants?

Studies show that houseplants lift our spirits and improve air quality. Not bad benefits at all!

### Where do you buy houseplants?

Most garden centers and home improvement stores will have a houseplant section. Otherwise, you can look online. Also, many houseplants can be started from other houseplants by taking cuttings. So if you have a friend who has a lot of houseplants, just ask.

### With houseplants, is more better?

Well, this is really a personal preference, but if you're actually trying to improve the air quality, yes. More is better. You'll need a pretty hefty number of houseplants (usually ten or more) to do this.

### Do you have to worry about pets with houseplants?

Pets, kids, or anyone else who might eat houseplants—yes, you do have to worry. Many plants (not just houseplants) are poisonous or have poisonous parts to them. Do your research ahead of time. No one needs a hacking dog or cat.

# VEGGIES & HERBS

Growing your own fruits, veggies, and herbs definitely gives you a sense of accomplishment. Whether you start them from seed or get a head start by using plants, there's just something special about going out to the garden and harvesting something you grew from beginning to end. It seems to taste better, too. Veggie gardening is growing in popularity, and it's not hard to see why. Heirloom varieties are on the rise, giving us better flavor. Containers are also making it possible to grow veggies on patios and in other small spaces. If you've thought about growing veggies but haven't quite jumped in, now is the time. Or if you've mostly been growing a few tomatoes and peppers, then let's widen your range with these easy-to-grow options! As long as you can keep the garden weeded, you're nearly guaranteed success.

"What'd life be without homegrown tomatoes?"
—Guy Clark, "Homegrown Tomatoes" song

# TOMATOES

You just can't beat the flavor of a homegrown tomato, and in this day and age, you seriously have hundreds of varieties to choose from. Love heirlooms? You can get tomatoes in funky shapes and shades of purple, green, black, and orange. Looking to grow in containers? Tons of options have been cultivated for pots and patios. Want to cook or can with them? There are tomatoes that have been developed to produce high yield. Of course, you have to have miniature (cherry or grape) tomatoes in your garden, too, because nothing beats going outside and popping one directly into your mouth from the vine. Most tomato plants require about eight hours of sunlight a day, and they also need to be staked (or you can use a cage) so they don't flop over. www.burpee.com and www.rareseeds.com are good places to start to figure out what kind of tomatoes you want to grow.

## STATS

| Common Name | Tomatoes |
|---|---|
| Botanical Name | *Lycopersicon esculentum* |
| Season | Warm |
| Height | up to 6 feet |
| Spread | up to 6 feet |
| Spacing | 2 to 4 feet apart |
| Light Needs | Full sun |

## 🌱 GREEN THUMB TIP

Tomatoes are one of those plants that a lot of gardeners like to start by seed indoors. Here's the biggest tip—don't start your seeds too soon. You only need to start them about six weeks before you plant outside. Choose a spot with plenty of sunshine or else use a grow light. This way, they won't become "leggy" and die off before you get a chance to transplant them.

## ✓ TOP PICKS

Brandywine is a tried-and-true heirloom variety with great flavor, and it's easy to grow. Celebrity is an All-America Selections winner and is easy to find at many garden centers. Green Zebra is a smaller tomato with green and yellow stripes, which boasts wonderful flavor. Aunt Ruby's German Green is a delicious green variety. Black Cherry and Sweet 100 are both good options for mini tomatoes.

If you make pesto, you can save the extra by freezing it in plastic ice cube trays. Then you'll have little cubes to throw into your soups and other hot meals in winter.

# BASIL

## PROFILE

If you're going to grow tomatoes, then you might as well grow basil, too. These are great companion plants. They are also delicious together—just throw some basil leaves with cherry tomatoes and fresh mozzarella on a toothpick! One of the tricks to basil is pinching back the plants before they flower. This will keep the plants actively growing, and if you do this, you should be able to harvest about 4 to 6 cups of basil each week (as long as you have a few healthy plants). If you're producing too much, just freeze it, dry it, or make some pesto!

## STATS

| Common Name | Basil |
|---|---|
| Botanical Name | *Ocimum basilicum* |
| Season | Warm |
| Height | up to 2 feet |
| Spread | up to 2 feet |
| Spacing | 10 to 12 inches |
| Light Needs | Full sun |

## GREEN THUMB TIP

The smaller the leaves are on basil, the more flavorful they are. Use those leaves right away and don't wait for them to get too big.

## ✓ TOP PICKS

You're probably familiar with common sweet basil, but there are a few other options you might notice when you go to the garden center. Cinnamon basil has just the perfect hint of cinnamon flavor. Purple basil tastes a lot like the green, but it adds beautiful color in the garden. Thai basil can have a bit of a licorice flavor. Experiment a little by cooking with different varieties of basil you find at the farmers' market.

# RHUBARB

## PROFILE

This one could actually go in the perennial chapter, too. Hardy in zones 3 to 8, rhubarb deserves a spot in your flower bed, not just in your veggie garden. It's one of the earliest things to grow in spring, and has beautiful green leaves and pinkish red stalks. Once you harvest it, you'll definitely want to try your hand at making a rhubarb pie (or rhubarb strawberry pie).

## STATS

| Common Name | Rhubarb |
|---|---|
| Botanical Name | *Rheum × cultorum* |
| Season | Cool |
| Height | up to 3 feet |
| Spread | up to 4 feet |
| Spacing | 2 to 3 feet apart |
| Light Needs | Full sun to part shade |

## 🌱 GREEN THUMB TIP

If you're trying to establish rhubarb from seed for the first time, you need a little bit of patience. Plant in spring during the first year, and then just let it grow. Don't start harvesting until year two. Or if you start with two-year-old bare root plants, you can harvest in the first year.

ONLY EAT THE STALKS. THE LEAVES THEMSELVES CAN BE POISONOUS.

# ONIONS

## PROFILE

Everyone seems to have a different or favorite way to grow onions. Some gardeners are just looking to harvest them as scallions or as small onions for fresh or raw flavor. Others are looking to grow those large onions you can store to keep and use all winter. If you'd like some onions but don't need to plant dozens, consider tucking them in throughout your flower bed. They actually have attractive, grassy foliage, and you can harvest them as needed.

## STATS

| Common Name | Onions, scallions, bunching onions, green onions |
|---|---|
| Botanical Name | *Allium cepa var. cepa* |
| Season | Cool |
| Height | up to 3 feet |
| Spread | up to a foot |
| Spacing | Thin to 2 to 4 inches apart |
| Light Needs | Full sun |

## GREEN THUMB TIP

Like many veggies, it's important to have good weed control with onions. This way, the weeds don't crowd out the plants or take over. If you can stick to this one main rule, you'll have tons of onions to harvest each year.

# ASPARAGUS

## PROFILE

Asparagus is one of those investment crops. It might take a year or two to get them established in your garden before they really produce. But once they do—wow! You can get a bountiful harvest for many, many years. Make sure you find a good, permanent area to grow your asparagus since it will come back year after year. It's not exactly easy to relocate. Once the crop is done for the season, let the foliage grow. It can get quite tall and give good height and color to your garden.

## STATS

| | |
|---|---|
| Common Name | Asparagus |
| Botanical Name | *Asparagus officinalis* |
| Season | Cool |
| Height | up to 5 feet for most |
| Spread | up to 2 feet |
| Spacing | plant crowns 18 to 24 inches apart |
| Light Needs | Full sun to part shade |

## GREEN THUMB TIP

Asparagus is most tender when you harvest it small, plus harvesting promotes more growth. This is a good rule of thumb to use when buying asparagus at the farmers' market or store, too. Look for skinnier stalks.

## ✓ TOP PICKS

For the best, largest harvest, look for varieties like Jersey Giant, Jersey King, or Jersey Knight. You can also try the heirloom variety, Martha Washington. There's also a white variety of asparagus hitting gardens and farmers' markets and nurseries, so ask your local garden center about it or look to buy online.

# BEANS

## PROFILE

You can find entire books written about the different kinds of beans available!. You can get bush beans, which include everything from the French bean and wax bean to the traditional string or snap bean. Pole beans climb tall and high on a trellis or other support system, creating vertical interest in the garden. Some people like to grow bean teepees using branches or support to make a triangle shape. Beans grow best when you sow the seeds directly into the ground. They aren't plants you'll want to start inside first because they don't transplant very well. One advantage to pole beans (if you have the space) is they have a much larger harvest overall. However, bush beans provide a large variety to choose from.

## STATS

| Common Name | Bush beans and pole beans |
| --- | --- |
| Botanical Name | *Phaseolus vulgaris* |
| Season | Warm |
| Height | Bush beans grow a few feet tall and pole beans can get 10-plus feet |
| Spread | 2 to 3 feet for bush beans and much more for pole beans |
| Spacing | A couple inches apart in rows a couple feet apart |
| Light Needs | Full sun |

## ◉ GREEN THUMB TIP

Plant twice as many beans as you think you might need. Rabbits and deer love to eat this plant, so you'll want to have extra. Plus, if you get a big harvest, you can just freeze or can the extra.

## ✓ TOP PICKS

For a yellow pod (wax variety), look for Golden Butterwax or Golden Rod. For a green pod, look for Derby or Jade. For a cool and delicious heirloom, try Dragon's Tongue. And if you're looking for a pole bean, try Kentucky Wonder or Blue Lake.

# CHIVES

## PROFILE

Here's another one that could easily get categorized as a perennial. It's common to see this growing alongside tulips or daisies in the flower garden, and it is hardy in zones 3 to 8. It's also one of the earliest plants to grow and bloom in spring, producing beautiful puff ball–type flowers that are usually purple. Then once the flowers are done, the plant stays green through the rest of the season. To use chives, simply cut off the leaves or flowers and mince them up to add to your favorite dish. The flavor is a great mix between an onion and herbs.

## STATS

| Common Name | Chives |
|---|---|
| Botanical Name | *Allium schoenoprasum* |
| Season | Cool |
| Height | up to 2 feet |
| Spread | up to 1 foot |
| Spacing | 2 feet |
| Light Needs | Full sun to part shade |

## GREEN THUMB TIP

For a chive with a garlic flavor, try a different cultivar, *Allium tuberosum*. They tend to grow taller and produce white flowers.

# KALE

## PROFILE

In late summer or early fall, you'll likely start seeing kale hit the garden centers. This cool-season leafy green is a good autumn addition to your veggie garden, and you can harvest the leaves all the way into winter, if weather allows. Some gardeners don't even grow kale with intentions of eating it; they just like the color it adds to their fall garden or display. It does tend to be a bit tougher or more bitter than lettuce, so it's a good one to grow if you want to mix it in with other greens versus eating it alone.

## STATS

| | |
|---|---|
| Common Name | Kale |
| Botanical Name | *Brassica oleracea* var. *acephala* |
| Season | Cool |
| Height | up to 3 feet |
| Spread | up to 3 feet |
| Spacing | Plant 1 inch apart but eventually thin to 12- or 18-inch spacing |
| Light Needs | Full sun to part shade |

## 🌼 GREEN THUMB TIP

Some gardeners and chefs claim the flavor of kale gets better as the weather gets colder. They even like when it's been "kissed" by a bit of frost. So if you're growing kale and you get a light snow, go ahead and harvest it. You might find that you like it more!

OVEN-BAKED KALE CHIPS ARE DELICIOUS AND HEALTHY!

# CUCUMBER

## PROFILE

You might think you don't have room for cucumbers, but don't write them off just yet. With a little creativity, like growing them up a trellis or planting a grouping in the middle of your flower garden, you can grow your cucumbers and eat them, too! There are two important things to remember when growing cucumbers. First, you shouldn't plant them until the chance of frost has definitely passed. Second, they need lots of water to get established early in the season. If you can do these two things, then you should get a great harvest!

## STATS

| Common Name | Cucumber |
|---|---|
| Botanical Name | *Cucumis sativus* |
| Season | Warm |
| Height | up to 6 feet if grown up a trellis |
| Spread | up to 6 feet |
| Spacing | Grows well on "hills" with a few plants on each hill, 3 to 5 feet apart |
| Light Needs | Full sun |

## 🌱 GREEN THUMB TIP

Many veggie plants, including cucumbers, benefit by changing the location where they are planted each year. This means that if you grow cucumbers in one location for a couple years, you'll want to eventually switch to a new location.

## ✓ TOP PICKS

Pickling cucumbers get 3 to 4 inches long and are good for both eating and making pickles. Slicing varieties are longer, about 7 to 8 inches. Vining and bush cucumbers are both popular garden options. Finally, burpless and seedless options are very popular for eating raw.

Dill often reseeds itself from one year to the next.

# DILL

## PROFILE

Dill is a hidden gem in the herb world. You just have to decide whether you want to plant it in your flower garden or veggie and herb garden. It's a host plant to the black swallowtail butterfly, so you're definitely helping the butterfly population when you choose to grow it. (Many other beneficial insects love it, too.) Another huge benefit of dill is that you can use it for pickling. If you do any pickling at all, there's nothing like being able to go out into the garden and snip off your very own dill to add to the jar instead of buying it at the store or using the dried kind.

## STATS

| Common Name | Dill |
|---|---|
| Botanical Name | *Anethum graveolens* |
| Season | Warm |
| Height | up to 5 feet |
| Spread | up to 3 feet |
| Spacing | 18 inches apart |
| Light Needs | Full sun |

### 🌀 GREEN THUMB TIP

If you want to have a continual harvest of dill for all your pickling needs, then plant new seeds every few weeks from early spring to early summer. This will ensure you always have a fresh supply of dill to add to your canning jars.

# RADISH

## PROFILE

The radish is like the epitome of a cool-season veggie. It does best in almost chilly, damp conditions. This is why you'll see lots of radishes in spring. One of the best traits of this veggie is that it has a very short harvest! You can plant radishes and then be eating them just four to six weeks later. You'll want to focus on other veggies in summer, but then as temperatures start to cool again in fall, add some more radishes to the garden for an autumn harvest.

## STATS

| Common Name | Radish |
|---|---|
| Botanical Name | *Raphanus sativus* |
| Season | Cool |
| Height | up to 2 feet |
| Spread | up to 1 foot |
| Spacing | 1 inch apart in rows spaced 1 foot apart |
| Light Needs | Full sun to part shade |

## 🌀 GREEN THUMB TIP

To keep a long harvest, start planting in early spring and then plant new ones every week or two. This way, you'll get to enjoy radishes for weeks instead of just one harvest and being done.

# OREGANO

PROFILE

## PROFILE

Oregano is one of the most popular herbs grown for cooking. Best of all, it requires almost no maintenance, so you can just add it to your garden and let it do its thing. A lot of gardeners like using oregano as a companion plant because they say it helps repel insects that go after beans and broccoli. It sure can't hurt to try! You can find a lot of different varities of oregano, including ones that are hot and spicy or sweet. Definitely read the plant label on oregano—it'll likely have a good description right there.

## STATS

| | |
|---|---|
| Common Name | Oregano |
| Botanical Name | *Origanum vulgare* |
| Season | Warm |
| Height | up to 2 feet |
| Spread | up to 2 feet |
| Spacing | Seed a few inches apart and eventually thin to 1 foot apart |
| Light Needs | Full sun |

## 🌿 GREEN THUMB TIP

The best time to harvest oregano is when it's no more than 6 inches tall. This will give you the best flavor overall.

Note that spinach and arugula are both completely different from lettuce.

# LETTUCE

## PROFILE

"Plant it early, and plant it late." This is another one of those veggie crops that likes the cool weather, so you can grow it in spring and then plant another crop in fall. In general, most types of lettuce have a shallow root system, so it's an excellent candidate for growing in containers or around the patio. It can take some shade, too. You will find dozens of lettuce options in an array of sizes and colors at your local garden center and farmers' markets.

## STATS

| Common Name | Lettuce |
| --- | --- |
| Botanical Name | *Lactuca sativa* |
| Season | Cool |
| Height | up to 2 feet |
| Spread | up to 2 feet |
| Spacing | Plant 1 inch apart and thin to 12 to 18 inches |
| Light Needs | Full sun to part shade |

### 🌑 GREEN THUMB TIP

It really is best to try a lot of different lettuce varieties. Everyone likes something different, so designate a lettuce area and see what works. In addition, be sure to harvest at the right time when the lettuce is still on the small size and tender. It tastes much better this way.

### ✓ TOP PICKS

When it comes to lettuce, there are five main types. Take a look.

1. Looseleaf. It's easy to grow and one of the earliest ones you can plant.

2. Butterhead. Known for excellent flavor.

3. Romaine. Takes longer to harvest but can tolerate some warm weather.

4. French. Good for a summer harvest.

5. Crisphead. It's like iceberg and takes the longest to harvest.

# MICROGREENS

## PROFILE

Microgreens have been trending the past few years, and it's easy to see why! Basically, they're these little sprouts from veggie or flower seeds harvested when they are just a few inches tall. Microgreens are so popular because those little greens pack a huge punch of flavor and nutrients. Because you harvest them so small, all those nutrients are really concentrated, so they're really good for you! Best of all, you can grow them anywhere you want: inside, outside, in a cardboard box, or in your garden. You just plant the seeds, wait a couple of weeks, and then harvest! Add them to your salad or favorite dish.

## STATS

| Common Name | Microgreens |
| --- | --- |
| Season | Year-round |
| Height | a few inches |
| Spread | a few inches |
| Spacing | Sprinkle around, no need to thin out |
| Light Needs | Sun to shade |

## 🌱 GREEN THUMB TIP

You can buy a special blend of microgreen seeds if you want. Otherwise, just use the extra seeds of lettuce or sunflowers you have around the garden. It really is that easy!

# MINT

## PROFILE

This is truly a fail-proof herb. In fact, it's such a sure thing, it's even considered aggressive by some gardeners, who can't get rid of it. There is an easy fix, though: keep it contained! Either grow your mint in a pot, or make sure it's in a flower bed bordered by a sidewalk or concrete. Then you can enjoy the benefit and fragrance of mint without having to worry about it taking over your garden!

## STATS

| Common Name | Mint |
|---|---|
| Botanical Name | *Mentha* |
| Season | Warm |
| Height | up to 2 feet |
| Spread | up to 2 feet |
| Spacing | 1 to 2 feet apart |
| Light Needs | Full sun |

### 🌿 GREEN THUMB TIP

You can find lots of different mint varieties, including apple or pineapple mint (*Mentha suaveolens*), peppermint (*Mentha × piperita*) and citrus mint (*Mentha × piperita var. citrate*). Also, don't forget to grow a regular mint so you can make mojitos or mint juleps!

IN SOME AREAS, MINT IS CONSIDERED A PERENNIAL.

# POTATOES

Keep a few things in mind when it comes to potatoes, and you'll be good to go. First of all, they like soil that is more acidic, which is different than most veggies, so make adjustments as needed (ask someone at your garden center for help). Next, they like well-drained soil, and it's good to keep them watered consistently. Then that's pretty much it! Now you just need to pick out which kind you want! Big, small, purple, gold, white—there are plenty to choose from!

## STATS

| Common Name | Potatoes |
|---|---|
| Botanical Name | *Solanum tuberosum* |
| Season | Warm |
| Height | up to 3 feet |
| Spread | up to 3 feet |
| Spacing | 8 to 12 inches apart |
| Light Needs | Full sun |

## 🌀 GREEN THUMB TIP

Grow potatoes in containers! Make sure you use extra large containers, or if you want to be thrifty, grow potatoes in a big cardboard box. It's free, and it will easily come apart when it's time to dig in and harvest the potatoes.

## ✓ TOP PICKS

Try Dark Red Norland. Yukon Gold is a pretty traditional potato popular among many gardeners. For unique varieties that have good flavor, look for Adirondack Blue (dark purple), French Fingerling, and German Butterball.

# RASPBERRY

## PROFILE

Every veggie and herb chapter needs a fruit in it, and raspberries are definitely one of the easiest to grow. You will need some space, though. They tend to grow tall and multiply like crazy, but this could be a good thing! In a couple years, you could have a huge raspberry patch. Once they get established, you'll want to offer support with a fence or stakes.

## STATS

| Common Name | Raspberries |
|---|---|
| Botanical Name | *Rubus idaeus* |
| Season | Warm and cool |
| Height | up to 8 feet |
| Spread | up to 2 feet |
| Spacing | 3 feet apart in rows 8 feet apart |
| Light Needs | Full sun |

## GREEN THUMB TIP

There are two main types of raspberries—summer-bearers and ever-bearers. Both should be planted in early summer, but the first bears one crop. And the other will have two crops, one in summer and the other in fall. One isn't necessarily better than the other. It's more important to grow a good cultivar that works in your area. Inquire at your local garden center, and they should be able to help you.

# ROSEMARY

## PROFILE

Grow rosemary for its wonderful scent. Grow it for making your own tea. Grow it for cooking. Rosemary has a wide range of uses, so it's easy to see why it's one of the most popular herbs among gardeners. It's good to grow indoors in fall or winter, too—when you need a little bit of green but gardening season is still weeks away. If you do grow rosemary indoors or move it from outside to inside for the winter, be sure to give it plenty of light.

## STATS

| Common Name | Rosemary |
| --- | --- |
| Botanical Name | *Rosmarinus officinalis* |
| Season | Warm |
| Height | up to 4 feet |
| Spread | up to 4 feet |
| Spacing | a foot apart |
| Light Needs | Full sun |

## GREEN THUMB TIP

If your rosemary got big and lanky during the summer, it might not be the best candidate to move inside for winter. If this is the case, take a cutting instead. It's a good challenge, and is relatively easy to do.

159

You can get crazy high yields when it comes to squash. For instance, winter squash can produce as much as 75 pounds in 100 square feet.

# SQUASH

The first thing to know about squash is the two main types—summer and winter. Summer is mostly known for zucchini (look for that later on in this chapter). So let's take a minute to focus on winter squash, which includes acorn and butternut, among others. With *winter* in the name, you can probably guess this squash doesn't produce until late in the season. This is good! This means there's no reason to try to start seeds indoors or early. Just take your time and get it going after most of your other veggies are planted for the season. It can take a while for it to mature, so you'll have a nice harvest in late summer, fall, or early winter.

## STATS

| Common Name | Squash, winter squash, acorn squash, butternut squash |
|---|---|
| Botanical Name | *Cucurbita maxima* is most common, but check for others |
| Season | Warm |
| Height | up to 3 feet |
| Spread | up to 15 feet |
| Spacing | Plant a few inches apart and thin to 1 to 2 feet |
| Light Needs | Full sun |

## GREEN THUMB TIP

If you don't have the space for squash, don't worry—it is still possible to grow it. Try growing it up a trellis. You can also get inexpensive trellis strings that go over poles. This way, you can still grow this sprawling plant, even if you don't have the ground space.

## ✓ TOP PICKS

For butternut squash, look for these cultivars—Bugle, Ponca Baby, and Zenith. For acorn squash, look for Table Ace, Carnival, and Tuffy. For buttercup, look for Autumn Cup or Sweet Meat.

# SWEET CORN

## PROFILE

Some gardeners say sweet corn is a little picky about soil. No big deal—just add some compost at the beginning of the season to get you started. (Actually, this is a good idea for all areas of your garden in general.) Once you get sweet corn growing, it's like the star of the garden. It grows tall very fast, which can really make your little veggie garden look active and productive. Not everyone wants to save space for sweet corn because it does grow so tall and big; however, if you plant it along the back of your garden, it frames up the space nicely, and you'll get corn, too!

## STATS

| Common Name | Sweet corn |
|---|---|
| Botanical Name | *Zea mays* |
| Season | Warm |
| Height | up to 6 feet or more |
| Spread | up to 30 feet |
| Spacing | plant in groups, eventually thin to 8 to 12 inches apart |
| Light Needs | Full sun |

## 🌑 GREEN THUMB TIP

This is one of the easiest plants to grow in the garden because you sow the seeds directly into the ground. Plant several in one area, and eventually thin them out. Look for both traditional yellow varieties to grow as well as bicolor options.

# SUGAR SNAP PEA

## PROFILE

Peas are a warm season crop, but they're one of the earliest. Sow seeds directly into the ground as soon as you can work them into the soil. They're going to grow best if you put them in full sun, but they will take a little bit of shade if needed. The best time to eat peas (like most veggies) is immediately after you harvest them. Really, even eating them right there in the garden seems to make them taste better. You can find others in the pea family besides sugar snap, but these are the best because you can eat them raw (shell and all) or throw them on a salad.

## STATS

| | |
|---|---|
| Common Name | Peas, sugar snap peas |
| Botanical Name | *Pisum sativum* |
| Season | Warm |
| Height | Usually just 1 or 2 feet |
| Spread | up to 1 foot |
| Spacing | 2 to 4 inches apart |
| Light Needs | Full sun to part shade |

## 🌿 GREEN THUMB TIP

You definitely want to overplant when it comes to peas. Start sowing seeds early in spring, and then add new ones every couple weeks. This will ensure a long harvest in summer!

# ZUCCHINI

When most gardeners are talking about squash, they're likely referring to the resilient, easy-to-grow, high-producing zucchini. But don't forget the other squash in this family, which includes zucchini, yellow, scalloped, and pattypan squash. All are planted in late spring and should produce quite well for you throughout the summer. Plant in a space that will give it plenty of room—remember, squash can really sprawl. You could even plant it on a mound in the middle of your flower garden and let it grow between the blooms.

## STATS

| Common Name | Zucchini, squash, summer squash |
| --- | --- |
| Botanical Name | *Cucurbita pepo* |
| Season | Warm |
| Height | up to 3 feet |
| Spread | up to 4 feet |
| Spacing | Plant a few inches apart and thin to 1 to 2 feet |
| Light Needs | Full sun |

## GREEN THUMB TIP

Don't plant squash too early. It's pretty sensitive to cold, so if you do this, one late frost can kill it. It's an easy one to grow from seed. Just make sure to thin it out once the plants sprout.

## ✓ TOP PICKS

If you like yellow squash, look for cultivars like Seneca, Sunburst, or Yellow Crookneck. If you like zucchini, try Gold Rush or Midnight Zucchini.

HARVEST SQUASH ON THE SMALL SIDE. IF YOU LET IT GET TOO BIG, THE FLAVOR ISN'T AS GOOD.

# BEETS

Beets are gorgeous specimens, but they tend to puzzle a lot of people. What do you do with them? How do you use them? Don't let them intimidate you. They are one of the most versatile plants in the garden because you can use the roots for baking, sautéing, etc. Plus, you can eat the greens on top. You can find beets in several different colors, but red is the most common (after all, where do you think the term *beet red* came from?). They are one of the easiest plants to grow in a veggie garden—especially with kids!

## STATS

| Common Name | Beets |
|---|---|
| Botanical Name | *Beta vulgaris subsp. vulgaris* |
| Season | Cool |
| Height | up to 2 feet |
| Spread | up to 2 feet |
| Spacing | 12 to 18 inches apart |
| Light Needs | Full sun to part shade |

## 🌀 GREEN THUMB TIP

Plant more beets than you actually need. Then thin the plants out once they reach 4 to 5 inches tall.

# FAQS ON VEGGIES

## Are all the ones in this chapter really veggies?

So, are you questioning whether tomatoes are fruits or veggies? And what about raspberries? Those are definitely fruits, and they're here in the veggies chapter! What's up with that?! Yeah, yeah—let's not get technical. It's the veggie chapter, but the range is wide.

## Do you have to have sunshine for all veggies?

The short answer is yes. It's hard to grow veggies without a good source of sunshine, and it's really the number-one reason that most people fail. Some veggies can take less sun than others, but you do need to look for a sunny spot in your yard before you dive into growing veggies.

## Can you really save money growing your own?

Absolutely. Do a side-by-side investment test sometime. Since so many veggies can be grown from seed, this is one of the best investments you can make in a single summer. Case in point—think about buying a pack of tomato seeds for $3 at the most. This could yield ten gallons or more of tomatoes! Great investment.

## Should you use seeds or plants?

This is a personal preference. Some people love the challenge of starting seeds indoors before the growing season. Plus, it saves money. However, others like the convenience of starting with plants—it's a little bit easier overall, and you don't have to invest so much time. So it's your call. Garden centers offer both. It's okay to mix it up, too.

Favorite Plant:
Pineapple Sage

Favorite Plant:
Purple Coneflower

Favorite Plant:
Sunflower

# ABOUT THE AUTHOR

Stacy Tornio is the former editor of the national gardening magazine, *Birds & Blooms*. In recent years, she's been a master gardener and writes about gardening for national websites and magazines. Stacy is also the author of more than ten books about animals, nature, and outdoor topics, including the kids' gardening book Project Garden and the award-winning book, *The Kids' Outdoor Adventure Book*. Stacy strongly believes in sharing her love of gardening with kids. She and her own two kids, Jack and Annabelle, love growing fruit, veggies, and all kinds of flowers. Check out their favorite picks below! You can learn more about Stacy at www.destinationnature.com

# PLANT INDEX

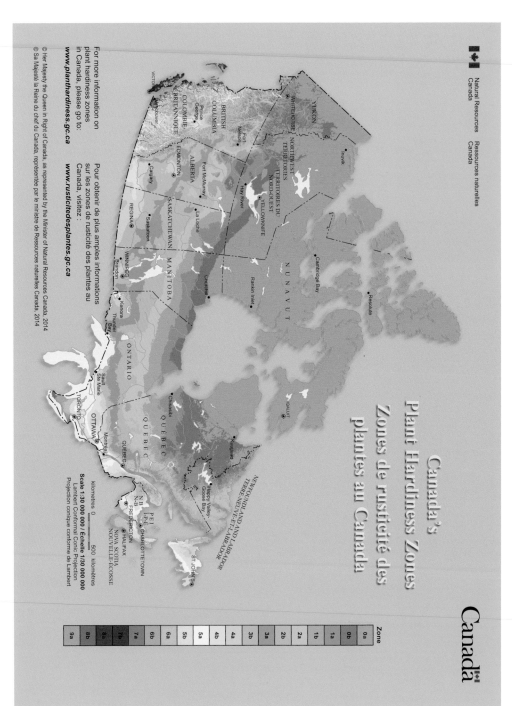

Natural Resources Canada
Ressources naturelles Canada

Canada

# Canada's Plant Hardiness Zones
# Zones de rusticité des plantes au Canada

For more information on plant hardiness zones in Canada, please go to:
**www.planthardiness.gc.ca**

Pour obtenir de plus amples informations sur les zones de rusticité des plantes au Canada, visitez :
**www.rusticitedesplantes.gc.ca**

Kilomètres 0                    500 kilomètres
**Scale 1:30 000 000 / Échelle 1/30 000 000**
Lambert Conformal Conic Projection
Projection conique conforme de Lambert

Zone

| 0a |
| 0b |
| 1a |
| 1b |
| 2a |
| 2b |
| 3a |
| 3b |
| 4a |
| 4b |
| 5a |
| 5b |
| 6a |
| 6b |
| 7a |
| 7b |
| 8a |
| 8b |
| 9a |

# NOTES